Better Words for Better Living
Power Words to Change Your Life

Better Words for Better Living
Power Words to Change Your Life

Bill Becker

TransMedia Press
Philadelphia, PA

© William Becker, 2017

All rights reserved. Except as permitted under the U.S copyright Act of 1976, no part of this publication may be reproduced, distributed, or transmitted in any form by any means, or in a database or retrieval system without prior permission of the author or publisher.

Book & Cover Design
Benson E. Fishman

ISBN 978-0-9820255-3-6

TransMedia Press is an imprint of
TransMedia Publishing Group

TransMedia Press
Philadelphia, PA

Dedication

Dedicated to my beloved wife of 11 years who recently went to heaven. Much too soon and too young, to you darling Eleanor, who gave me much pleasure and joy throughout our short time together. She made me a better person and was always the first to think of others, for whatever the reason. Even when she was taken from the hospital to home by Medical Transport just a couple of days before she passed, she whispered, because the nasty beast (cancer) had taken her voice; "Make sure you give them a tip." This is who she was and she will always live in my heart. A new star shines in the heavens and her name is Eleanor. Thank you my dear Sigi for sharing your love of humanity and all things living, especially me.

Your loving husband Bill.

Contents

Achieve	1
Attitude	2
Beautiful	5
Best	7
Comfortable	10
Compliment	13
Decorate	15
Dignity	17
Engaging	19
Enthusiasm	21
Friendly	23
Fun	25
Glad	28
Great	30
Happy	32
Helping	34
Initiate	36
Indicate	38
Join	40
Joy	43
Kind	45
Kiss	47
Laugh	49
Love	51
More	53
Muster	55
Necessary	58

Nice	61
Outstanding	63
Okay	65
Patience	68
Play	70
Quaint	72
Quest	75
Regard	78
Respect	81
Smile	84
Success	87
Terrific	91
Tremendous	93
Understanding	96
Utmost	98
Valor	100
Visionary	102
Welcome	104
Wonderful	106
Xenial	108
X-factor	110
Yes	112
Young	114
Zeal	117
Zenith	119
Some Final words	121
The Last Word	123
About the Author	125

Introduction

Wow really, really tough title to write about with some authority, but here I go. Long ago a poet once wrote, "A word once writ cannot be altered and can change a life for the good or for the worse." We all have this power; the power to use words "for the good or for the worse." All we have to do is discover the power within each of us and become one with it. And since you already own your Power Within, once you recognize it, your next step is to utilize your personal power to realize the best results for yourself and others.

Unfortunately, many people fail to fully understand the power of their words simply because they have a severely limited vocabulary. An example of this can be found in prison systems throughout the United States. I mention this because many behavorial studies have demonstrated that when a person's vocabulary is expanded, especially by using more positive words, recidivism is drastically reduced. That means people in prisons have a much better chance of not returning just because of a marked improved in their ability to communicate more effectively by using more positive words. I'd love to place a copy of this book in every prison cell throughout the country in the hope it could inspire others to make positive life changes.

So, here I sit at my computer, with a "Thanks a Bunch" porcelain cup full of hot green tea. It's 90 plus degrees outside in July in South Jersey. I do have an overhead fan. Otherwise the sweat would drop off my forehead and eventually ruin my computer keyboard. I won't apologize for a sprinkling of spiritual and social justice comments throughout this book because I feel those topics are important to all of us. I also take a stab at humor, drawn from my many from personal experiences which I thought were humorous at the time.

If you are a movie buff like me, you'll find this little book all that much more enjoyable. In it, I refer too many of the popular movies and or plays I have seen. You don't have to be a movie person, but you may get caught up in the "why" people spend so much money seeing these "Feel good" shows.

There are a number of words that come to mind when I think of living just for today. "Attitude" is one of them. Words that you've spoken, read, or heard and listened to are very, very powerful. If you focus on that word at the deepest personal level, you will derive more satisfaction from your life simply by changing an attitude from the negative to the positive. Try it and see how easily it can work for you.

One of the books I still revel in is by Kahlil Gibran, an American poet of Lebanese descent. It's entitled, "The Treasured writings of Kahlil Gibran." Here's my paraphrase one of his many insightful quotes. "A word once writ "cannot be taken back by all the tears in eternity." Think about that! So be very careful about what you write. Try a google search for, "Kahlil Gibran quotes," and you'll find many more words that have the power to change lives.

You can have also have a lot of "fun" with written words. Just for your own amusement, think about a "fun" word that brings some delightful memories to your mind. Write it down and stare at it awhile, especially during times that aren't much fun. But never forget that you need to maintain a positive attitude, even when times could be better.

In this little book, I've included words that, in my experience, have shown to have a powerful and positive impact on people's lives. Use each of these words for a week and you'll see your life and those around you begin change in positive ways. You'll start to see things from a new and more optimistic perspective. To help you along, I've included a check box for each word so that you can track your daily progress.

Choosing a word for the week and puting it into practice will, little by little, change your life for the better. They don't have to be any particular order. I have put them in alphabetical arrangement to help you. Use them wherever you can. For example, doodle the word while you're talking on the phone while you're on hold. Just "thinking" of the word can help make your day brighter.

Here's a little game that I occasionally play with someone who has issues with "certain things." Use one of your weekly words in the conversations you have with the person and keep using it every time you are in his or her company. One of three things will occur: They will get frustrated that they have failed to in win you over to their way of thinking, especially if you keep saying, "Thank you for sharing". They may respond by saying, "I didn't look at it that way, you might be on to something." The third and best reply could be; "Wow what a great attitude."

Yes, in truth, you do have to do both the legwork

and mind work to help yourself or someone have a better day. as well. Try this. Suppose you are having one of those "down days." Choose a word from the book or try starting a book of your own. Either way, you'll own that word and will have given yourself the power you need for turning the day into a good one.

So let's get started. It'll be your best day ever. After all, you deserve a good day, every day. Let me also suggest that you write your word for the week as many times as you can. Make an effort to read the little comments and stories in these pages every day. Doing so will help you retain the words in your vocabulary.

Let's begin with "Achieve" because when you begin to utilize this little book on a weekly basis you will achieve an exceptional feeling of great self worth each time you think positively about your weekly word.

Bill Becker

> **Achieve:** a verb
> to accomplish, reach, get and realize
>
> *I am going to **achieve** my goal of completing the draft of this book during this long weekend; in order that I might help others think more positively about their lives on a daily and weekly basis.*

Who and where are the achievers? Take a long good look around. You may not notice at first, but The simple truth is you'll find achievers are everywhere including you. Yes - you!

Here's something for you to think about. Out of millions upon millions of little squiggly sperm cells, all it took was one of them to find the target and become you — a totally unique individual, a born achiever right out of the gate. It's truly a God given gift from the very beginning. Imagine surviving a million to one shot and emerging with a lifetime to achieve whatever you set your mind to do.

Each of us is imbued with God's mind, so as our first task in this new journey called life, let's begin to put it to good use by helping others.

Our imagination helps us generate and visualize ideas that we constantly think about. It's this process that stimulates us to take the necessary steps to transform those ideas to reality. imagination is what energizes us to achieve.

We all have choices to achieve good things or bad

Better Words For Better Living

things. We can be a Superhero like Superman, who was sent to earth from Krypton by his father Jorell, to do good and battle evil. That is why we love to read about him and watch movies about him. When we see him overcome impossible odds and triumph over evil, it makes us feel good.

And it also make us feel good when we think about the many things we achieved in our lives under difficult if not impossible odds. True, our accomplishments may have not been as grand as Superman's, but certainly, to us, they were no less important.

Maybe we can't "leap tall buildings at a single bound or fly faster than a speeding bullet," all of us can, nevertheless, achieve something good and worthwhile and lasting.

Utilizing this word for a week will help you achieve your dreams along with your footwork.

Use this word everyday for a week. Check yourself below.						
Sun	M	T	W	T	F	Sat

> **Attitude:** noun
> way of thinking and or behaving
>
> *Eleanor has a great attitude because she always greets others with a great big warm smile and a very pleasant "hello."*

Attitude has many meanings, but our focus is on positive ideas. Unfortunately, we are constantly being bombarded with 40-50 negative statements for every positive statement or action throughout the course of a normal day.

For many words, including attitude, it's the inference that really counts. Here's a good example: "**You have an attitude**," with a heavy emphasis on *"attitude."* You know what it really means here and that it infers a mean or nasty attitude. In spite of the speaker's outlook, there's no mistaking the meaning as being negative in this context.

You know what is fun? When you steer the attitude of someone or maybe a group of people having a "bad hair" day from the negative to the positive.

It's not that difficult because an attitude, positive or negative, is contagious. You can guide and direct the person or group to a different line of thinking. I like to gradually ease them into a positive mind set by changing the subject, sometimes quite blatantly. This is especially effective when it comes to negative

Better Words For Better Living

racial comments or knocking someone because of a handicap.

But easing in isn't the most direct approach. One of my favorite approaches to open with a thought provoking question such as, "What do you think of our current educational system?" Almost everyone has an opinion on that topic and often it's not a very flattering one. However, it does change the focus.

The truth is, most of the nation's teachers are under paid and disrespected. But there's no doubt that teachers have positive and negative influences on students' lives. Follow up that question with a quote or short story of how a teacher positively changed a student's life. I am sure you can come up with at least one and I guarantee you'll come up with many stories.

I have a lot of fun doing this though you need to have a new story from time to time. Often you can steer someone away from a following the "herd" attitude to become a strong advocate for a more positive point of view.

Remember, a different attitude can change lives for the better. Also, remember that a positive engaging attitude leaves a beautiful impression on others.

Use this word everyday for a week. Check yourself below.						
Sun	M	T	W	T	F	Sat

Bill Becker

> **Beautiful:** adjective
> good looking, gorgeous, stunning and exquisite
>
> *I am sitting here in my room looking at the changing of the once all green trees into beautiful autumn colors of red, rust and gold.*

Costa Rica is a beautiful country populated with spiritual and physically beautiful people. Beautiful is mainly attributed to women though according to some women, there are some beautiful men.

A piece of art might be termed beautiful. The word is often used as slang. My son-in-law uses beautiful as slang quite frequently. For example, if one of my grandsons scores a hockey goal, he would say "**Beautiful.**" I have, at least once, and most likely only once, hit a beautiful shot during a golf outing.

I have traveled extensively. In many countries the locals welcome you in their own language with such phrases like, "Welcome to our beautiful country." I like this word and in fact it is one of my favorites because it's simple, self descriptive and it is easily translatable in almost any culture.

On a recent trip to Puntacana in the Dominican Republic we stayed at a beautiful resort. Somehow, I could not help thinking that just a mere 150 miles or so away from this beautiful country, the people of Haiti are not living such beautiful lives and I am reminded that one of our most important quests is to help all people experience what beautiful is. As I work on this manuscript, for this my third personal development book, out of my window, here at Weston Monastery in scenic Vermont where I often go to write, I can see a beautiful mountain landscape.

All the people who come here seek a beautiful experience of serenity and quiet. Over the past 25 years, I have brought many friends and relatives here. They do not know what to expect other than what I've told them which is it's a beautiful environment that they must experience.

The word has a subtle effect. Combine that effect with a passion for all people and it will aid you in your quest for a happier life. Be the best you can be by being beautiful from the inside.

"Beautiful" things are all around you as long as you're open to seeing them.

Use this word everyday for a week. Check yourself below.							
Sun	M	T	W	T	F	Sat

> **Best:** adjective
> A favorable outcome! Being better than anyone or anything
>
> *People seem to respond more favorably when you bring out the best in them by giving them a positive compliment.*

Now there is a powerful "success" oriented word. We all strive to be the best we can be if we expect to succeed in any endeavor. We all want to perform at our peak of effectiveness but do we have the discipline to do this. Hmm, a very interesting concept, "have the discipline." Even though we all have the ability to do our best we really have to "get to it," or as a popular comedian said, "Get 'er done!"

In baseball, the best players get paid the most. The best might only be one base hit a week more than the second best, but the difference between the best and second best converts into millions of dollars. What does one have to do to become the best? It's not just talent. It's hard "get 'er done" work - batting practice and more batting practice, especially when others are still sleeping or otherwise wasting time.

How about basketball players. I read that one basketball player practiced 8 hours each day and some of that time was used to actually shoot from the first row of the arenas' seats. This helped make him the best of his era, see if you can guess he had blond hair and was on a championship team, He wasn't satisfied until he was better than his teammates and that made him the best.

You say you are too old? How about Mick Jagger of the Rolling Stones. He's older than me but he and the group still practice 6-8 hours each and every day. That's why the Rolling stones are still the best classic rock band in the world and still going strong. It takes hard work to be the best, but it's worth it.

One of the best stories I can think of to illustrate this idea is from a movie, *"Men of Honor"* with Cuba Gooding Jr and Robert DeNiro. Cuba was a sharecroppers son who joins the US Navy and strives to become a Navy Rescue diver in spite of only having a 7th grade education.

Based on a true story, it's one of the best movies I've ever seen. In fact, I thought it was so good, I watched it twice in one sitting. I can't remember a time I sat through a movie twice. I'd rate it in my top five movies of all time. Though I thought it was a "macho, macho man" flick, my wife got into it as well. This surprised me since she mostly always likes "chick flicks."

DeNiro, of course, was the strict drill master who put Cuba through a myriad of very tough training maneuvers. The story takes place in the late 50's. It was a time when prejudice was everywhere, especially in the military. DeNiro's character was a typical, down home southern redneck, and if that wasn't bad enough, DeNiro's commanding officer was even worse.

The film wasn't just about racial injustice. It was about two men. DeNiro's character has an epiphany, causing him to change his thinking when he realizes that no matter what color, race or gender you were, we were all equal.

Cuba's character is driven by pure persistence. His goal is to be the best Navy Diver there ever was and the first black diver as well. In the beginning, Cuba's father told to be the best he could be, to never give up and never aspire to be like him. He listened.

Watching this movie was like reading a great book that you never wanted to end. It's an inspiring story that I guarantee you will enjoy immensely. It will leave you with a wonderful day cherishing all its moral and spiritual values.

Regardless of age, gender or color, we can all feel comfortable in our own skin if we know who are and have confidence in our ability to meet the challenges at hand.

Use this word everyday for a week. Check yourself below.						
Sun	M	T	W	T	F	Sat

Better Words For Better Living

> **Comfortable:** adjective relaxed, well-off
>
> *When I bring friends, relatives or associates to the Priory in Vermont for a retreat, the Brothers welcome us and make us feel very comfortable.*

I like this word. In fact, I am very comfortable with this word. I like being in a state of physical or mental comfort; contented and undisturbed. Being comfortable is more than merely adequate or sufficient; a comfortable salary, a comfortable relationship is nice as is a pleasant smile. This word goes the extra mile in satisfaction in many areas of emotions. That old worn chair is very comfortable in a physical sense and maybe from an emotional perspective as well. Especially, if a deceased loved one once sat in the chair. Think about the word and it will generate comfortable memories of pleasant times even though you sorely miss that person. Overall, it will bring you comfort knowing he or she was once with you.

What is comfortable? Isn't it a matter of individual choice? What is comfortable for you may not be for me, even though I may be convinced that it is comfortable. So here's a very short, comfortable story from my earlier days.

One of the advantages of living as long as I have is that I have lots and lots of experiences to share. I was in my early thirties and had a very comfortable position with the City of brotherly love or as others (not me) would call it shove instead of love. Yes, I had a corner office overlooking city hall, a city car, several eager to succeed underlings ready to jump to my requests. Of course, one of the real comforts was my salary. It was just under the salaries of those holding the top positions even though I was only number 4 in the pecking order of nearly 300 mostly patronage employees.

Even though it was a political appointment, my group/team was known as "Becker's grist mill." This was because I actually held my people accountable and expected them to work at least 6 out of the 8 hours they were getting paid for. You would seem to think they might resent me, however unbeknownst to me they actually admired my work ethic…thanks dad! They were not necessarily comfortable with the time they needed to put in, but that is another story for another time.

I was quite comfortable until that fateful day. That was the day when a new mayor was elected causing my comfort level to decrease enormously. My wife's comfortable feelings dropped even faster when she saw my name in the Philadelphia Inquirer announcing that I and several top level employees were fired… oh well! But, you see, oddly enough, that was the precisely the day when my comfort level actually rose! Why you ask? Because I knew, yes, I knew that

Better Words For Better Living

I would never work for anyone but myself. Never under any circumstances would I work for anyone but myself, right up until the day our maker calls us to account. And that was over thirty plus years ago. Even today, I feel the same way. And, thank God, I am still very comfortable with that decision.

This is my version of comfortable and I hope you got a little comfort from my true story. But the best is yet to come. Unlike many former employees, I was actually complimented by many of the people who worked there because I helped them feel they were really doing a service for the public instead of just being political hacks.

Use this word everyday for a week. Check yourself below.							
Sun	M	T	W	T	F	Sat

> **Compliment:** noun (praise, tribute, accolade) verb (flattern admire, butter up)
>
> *When we compliment someone sincerely, we sometimes help them feel good about themselves.*

Compliment is a great word, but take care when using it. Sometimes, if a compliment isn't delivered properly, it can come off as insincere or as a superficial form of flattery.

I have a good friend named of Jim. At a recent event, I made what I thought was a complimentary comment about his hair, and how I wished I my hair as thick as his. He was a tad taken back. Though I was sure he knew I had meant it in a positive sense, he could not take a compliment. Instead, he replied, "I have to get a haircut." Maybe the compliment took him off guard. I don't really know. Then again, maybe I am being too analytical. As with all words, we need to think through how our complimentary remarks might be received.

Everyone's heard the expression, "imitation is the greatest form of flattery" and to some extent, it's true. In my younger and more impressionable days I tried to imitate the "cool youthful look" of the popular actor James Dean. Later, as I matured, I tried to imitate John Wayne's walk so I would look more masculine or manly.

Better Words For Better Living

But the real truth is that the best compliment you can give yourself, is by being yourself simply because that is who you are. You wake up everyday day as yourself, not John Wayne or someone else. How about waking up and complimenting yourself by saying your name and telling yourself this is going to be one of if not your best days ever. Now, add to that a reminder to yourself to compliment at least one person during the day. It's a lot easier than you'd think. Begin with the closest person to you, your spouse or significant other or a friend.

But here is one that a little tougher—compliment someone you may have had some difficulty with in the past or present. That might positively change both your attitudes about each other.

You might say, "I don't particularly share all your philosophy, but you have great taste in clothing. Where did you get that coat?" Try it. You might like complimenting people.

One of the greatest giver of compliments was Napoleon. He was lavish in his praise for his men and decorated them by awarding medals for achieving even the smallest success.

Use this word everyday for a week. Check yourself below.							
Sun	M	T	W	T	F	Sat	

Bill Becker

> **Decorate:** verb: beautify, enhance, embellish, spruce up, award, honor
>
> *I wonder who our neighbor got to decorate their house.*

This a word that can be used in various ways. You can decorate a Christmas tree or spruce up a rental property to get it rented. But my favorite usage is related to "award" for an honor. I have a selfish reason. My son Kevin was decorated for his participation in the Gulf war as a United States Marine.

There are different types of honors. The highest, for an American military person, is being decorated by the President or Congress with The Medal of Honor. One of the nation's most decorated heroes was Audie Murphy. He received. the nation's highest award, the Medal of Honor, for killing and capturing the greatest number of the enemy during WWII. In fact, one of the best war movies and one that's high on my list, is "To Hell and Back," In it, Audie played himself. He was the most decorated marine for that WW2 conflict.

Getting back to my son. Kevin was stationed in 29 Palms, a marine base camp in California just outside of LA and San Diego being trained as a desert warrior in the armory division. He called me from there once just before being shipped out. During the conversation he said, "I can't stay on the phone long because there is long line of other guys waiting to call home. We've be called up to go to Saudi Arabia. He

Better Words For Better Living

asked me if it was all right to be scared. He told me that a lot of the boys were sick and could not even talk. I told him I did not raise a fool, and yes, he should be scared and that his best chance for staying alive was obeying the orders of his leaders, and most of all, do what is right in Gods eyes.

Kevin was there for almost a year and was a part of the vanguard that retook Kuwait. One of his duties was to clean out the enemies bunkers. No not with a broom, but with a grenade. Many soldiers would give a brief warning, then throw in the grenade into the bunker without waiting for the occupants to come out. Kevin crawled inside the bunkers where a group of enemy officers were praying with their prayer beads. He not only warned them, but showed them the grenade as well. Of course, they scurried out with their prayer beads in hand.

This did not go unnoticed. The enemy officers told their captors and the word went to the commanders. As a result of his heroic actions, Kevin was decorated by the United States Congress. That is one of my most treasured possessions. Kevin went in a boy and came out a man's man because he saved lives. This is a level of respect that can never be bought. He is and always will be my personal hero and earned that decoration in a difficult and dangerous conflict.

Use this word everyday for a week. Check yourself below.						
Sun	M	T	W	T	F	Sat

Bill Becker

> **Dignity:** noun: poise, self respect, self esteem, pride
>
> *The African lion walks with dignity through his domain as befits the king of the jungle.*

We all know many people who have real dignity, the kind you don't have to "put on." You might say that they carry themselves with a great deal self respect. It's what gives them genuine dignity, not the over-the-top kind. It what prevents them from being called snooty.

Can you think of someone with real dignity? Can you help someone become dignified? Does everyone have the power to change? Here's a secret. If you consistently tell someone that they look pretty or handsome and that they carry themselves with dignity even though they may at first look plain and may lack self confidence, they will begin to change.

I have seen it happen many times. One of my favorite plays and movies is "My Fair Lady," starring Audrey Hepburn. This is not fantasy played on the stage or screen, but real life portrayed as a fantasy. Think about that! I had the distinct pleasure of seeing the play in London and it was magnificent.

The premise of the story is quite simple. A street urchin, played by Audrey Hepburn, is ushered into a London home of a dignified couple on a bet that

Better Words For Better Living

one of the men claimed he could change the urchin into a dignified, respected lady while the other man claimed it was impossible because she had been born into this life style.

Of course you can guess what happened. The urchin was transformed into a dignified lady. The movie is definitely worthwhile to rent. Try watching it while working on this word as your weekly assignment. Even though it has its ups and downs just like life, it's a "feel good" entertaining production. After seeing it, you just may walk with your head held a tad or two higher, a self confident smile accompanied with a quicker step in your stride. There is hope for all of us to become as engaging as the star of this delightful movie.

Use this word everyday for a week. Check yourself below.							
Sun	M	T	W	T	F	Sat

Bill Becker

> **Engaging:** adjective: attractive, appealing, charming, winning
>
> *Many young people work hard at becoming "engaging" and make themselves attractive and appealing to win over a potential soul mate.*

The English language is one of, if not the hardest, for those who speak a different language to learn. That's because of its many words can have many meanings. But for our purpose, we're only going to focus on the positive meanings here. .

If my recollections of the romantic tales of the great lover Don Juan are correct, there's no doubt that he must have been a very engaging young man. Having achieved more than quite a few conquests, I can't imagine him not being super engaging.

Today, top athletes often represent good examples of recognizable engaging people. Arguably, the best basketball player in Philadelphia[s history, Wilt 'the Stilt' Chamberlain comes to mind for many who followed the team. His legendary achievement kept engaging his fan base in game after game. .

My late wife Mary ran into him one day, and I mean literally ran into him. She was coming out of work in a Philadelphia office building one late afternoon. Running to catch the subway through the underground maze beneath the office buildings, she

Better Words For Better Living

opened a door and ran smack into Wilt's stomach. Mary was five feet four. Wilt was seven feet one inch tall.

Mary always blushed a bit when she talked about this amusing encounter. Mary alway said he was very apologetic and charming, even though her rushing to catch the subway caused her to run into him. As the years, went by she would recall this run-in many times with great enthusiasm always ending with, "what an engaging man he was." People enthusiastically remember engaging people, Mary didn't have to work very hard at being engaging. It came quite naturally to her. Being engaging was just one of Mary's many gifts.

Use this word everyday for a week. Check yourself below.						
Sun	M	T	W	T	F	Sat

Bill Becker

> **Enthusiasm:** noun: eagerness, gust, zeal, interest, craze, passion
>
> *When I am focused on something that I truly want, my enthusiasm to accomplish my goal is unleashed like a grey hound at a dog race.*

It has been awhile since I viewed the movie Jerry McGuire. Though the plot was somewhat predictable, Cuba Gooding Jr's role as the start football player was one of the best. What I remember most, was his enthusiasm both on and off the screen.

Tom Cruise played the fast talking high powered agent who promised Cuba the moon including the rest of the universe to get him to sign with his agency. Tom was constantly pumping up Cuba to keep him on the payroll. Whether acting or not, Cuba comes across as a naturally enthusiastic personality. I won't give away any spoilers because this movie is just too good to miss. See it and you'll understand Cuba's enthusiasm. You probably only to see it once because Cuba's energy and enthusiasm is that powerful.

You see, if you are enthusiastic about your goal, enthusiasm can bring you many joyous moments, hours, days and even months. In fact, enthusiasm is contagious, in a good way. I am sure you must have experienced just how contagious enthusiasm can be. It's like a virus that easy to catch. If you're a sports

Better Words For Better Living

fan, you know that collective enthusiasm the fans have for their team can help motivate the players and spur them on to victory.

Putting aside his mis-directed off the field shenanigans, Pete Rose was one of the baseball's best players. Pete displayed boundless enthusiasm with every play, even if he knew he was going to be thrown out.

Modern day enthusiasm can be illustrated by Hunter Pence, who was acquired by my beloved Phillies in mid year 2011. Yes, the team was winning but something wasn't quite right, something was missing. Skill is not always the answer to winning, it must accompanied by large doses of enthusiasm. That's what Hunter brought to the Phillies, lots of high-energy enthusiasm. He's always a pleasure to watch even, when he strikes out.

Ryan Howard, known as the big stick, exudes a quiet type of enthusiasm. Hunter and Howard are always very friendly to all their fans, as are all the Phillies. This helps them on the field and off the field because the fans are there to see the enthusiastic friendly demeanor of their team.

Use this word everyday for a week. Check yourself below.						
Sun	M	T	W	T	F	Sat

Bill Becker

> **Friendly:** noun: favorably disposed; inclined to approve, help, or support
>
> *The teller at the bank greeted me with a most engaging, friendly smile and asked if I was having a good day*

Ah yes, a friendly bank. That's something we all want especially when we need one, which is almost always. But some banks seem to be unfriendly when you need them, especially when you need a loan. Nevertheless, many are favorably disposed to help.

Friendly can sometimes can be misinterpreted. In ancient days the extension of the hand, as we now know it (shake hands) was an indication that we had no weapons. Hence, extending of the hands is a friendly gesture. A kiss is another friendly gesture unless of course it's unwanted by the person receiving it. A smile is almost always a friendly gesture. Here's a short vignette of friendly from my personal experienced.

Friendly is where you are and what you think! Do you know people who have "friendly"faces? I know many. As a life coach counselor, I have a satellite office and am a "life coach counselor" at Starting Point in New Jersey where I meet the people I'm helping.

Our receptionist and all around helper is a most pleasant person. She always has smile on her face when I arrive and I am certain she has a friendly

Better Words For Better Living

smile for everyone. There are over 20 counselors at Starting Point whose sole purpose is to help those with emotional challenges that have caused stress or difficulties in their lives.

She reminds of one of my school teachers whom I liked very much because she was kind, friendly and most of all, understood my moods. In spite of being under pressure, every day when I come to my satellite office she has the same friendly attitude as the first time I met her. You know what people are really made of when you watch them under pressure or duress. I believe this lady has empathy for everyone and sympathizes with everyone's problems. She is comfortable to be around. I enjoy coming to my office knowing she'll be there to greet me.

She actually inspires me to become friendlier because she is an inspiration to all within 10 feet of her to become more friendly.

I yearn to have the natural friendly attitude like hers and work at it daily. So when you meet others like her, cherish them and catch their friendly attitudes. She helps make life better for me and everyone who sees her, which is why we all looked forward to coming to the office. She is a part of the "fun" of being alive. Thank you!

Use this word everyday for a week. Check yourself below.						
Sun	M	T	W	T	F	Sat

Bill Becker

> **Fun:** noun, verb, adjective amusement, amusing, behave playfully
>
> *Having a pinic would be fun!*

I heard some young people in their twenties and some in their thirties use the word "funner." Is there such a word? I couldn't find it in the dictionary but it does sound like it could be more fun than fun. "Funner," I guess it makes sense, but who cares if it makes sense if you're having more fun than fun. So part of a power play for a day is use the word fun or funner and focus on it.

I believe God has fun especially when I look in the mirror every morning. He must have had a blast conjuring me up. The older I get, the funnier I get too, so I guess God's funner days are infinite.

You can have more "funner" days in your life! What is "your" fun word? Write it down when you get up in the morning and before retiring at night. Make it big and bold! Carry it around with you and if someone sees it, tell him or her it is your fun word, then tell a fun story behind it. This will help them have a more pleasant day and you will feel good too. Every time they see or hear that word they will smile and think of you.

Here is one of my many fun memories. I volunteer at Inglis House in Philadelphia Pennsylvania,

Better Words For Better Living

formerly called the "Home for Incurables." Part of what I do is listen to the folks. Many are just left behind by their families who rarely visit. I always particularly select those who visited the least. I know you are thinking; what kind of fun would that be?

One of the residents, Danny, had severe MS. He was flat on his back on a gurney every time I visited with him. Danny could hardly talk, his voice more of a gasping whisper. But in spite of everything, Danny had a terrific sense of humor. "Pat and Mike" jokes by an Irish comedian, whose name escapes me, were his favorites.

He would tell me a new one each time I visited. Danny was only 35 years old, and I am sure he did not hear these jokes in Church. Well, it's possible he learned some from an Irish priest.

While on a 12-day pleasure trip to Ireland with my wife, we had the good fortune of seeing the same comedian who told nothing but "Pat and Mike "jokes. Coincidence? Perhaps. At the end of his gig, he announced that he had cassettes of his routine for sale at the back of the Pub. I purchased two.

Before my next visit with Danny, I stopped at the local electronics store and picked up an endless loop cassette player and earphones. I was very excited to tell him where I had been and that I'd seen a live performance of the "nameless" comedian. When I told him about it, he was thrilled. So I put the earphones on Danny and turned on the cassette player.

A huge smile crossed his face as he listened to some of Pat and Mike's "off color" jokes.

The tape was about 45 minutes long and because I had heard the routine many times, I decided to visit some other residents in the 300 plus home. I had left Danny to go about my rounds at around noon. Around 4 PM I had walked past Danny's room and suddenly remembered that the cassette player was an endless loop. If no one had turned it off, it would be still playing. To my amazement, Danny was still smiling and making little sounds when I walked in the room. I took the earphones off and apologized then bent down to hear what he was saying. He was not upset at all. He told me he had them all perfectly memorized and thanked me so much.

Unfortunately, some weeks later Danny passed on. I will never forget the fun both of us had retelling this story. I am sure Danny is somewhere in heaven smiling and recalling those "Pat and Mike" jokes.

Write down your "fun" word(s).

Use this word everyday for a week. Check yourself below.						
Sun	M	T	W	T	F	Sat

Better Words For Better Living

> **Glad:** adjective: happy, joyful, delighted, cheerful, thankful, pleased
>
> *I am glad my oldest son has become a top expert in his field.*

Though not a strong a word as I would like to use, it is however, very purposeful and direct as used in the sentence above. We have heard the word used in many different contexts, such as "glad tidings." Though tidings is not a word you often hear, it generally means "news." So when we think of "glad tidings," it's usually taken to mean "happy or cheerful" news.

A glad-hand usually means a "warm, hearty, enthusiastic" greeting. I like to use it in the right situations with the right people. But you've got to be careful. If taken the wrong way, glad-handing comes off as insincere, especially when applied to politicians.

When using the word glad, I generally think it needs another word in front of it to make it much stronger. For example, "I am really glad to see you!" It's like when a dog is really glad to see you, it wags its tail and huffs and puffs with excitement. That's what I like about dogs; they are almost always your friend. Even if you leave him for one minute and you have forgotten your cell phone, as I have many times, your dog will wag its tail and be really glad to see you once again.

Wouldn't it be a better world if people were like that? Maybe all of us should practice moving our posteriors just a tad when a loved one enters a room. Even if they don't see the movement, you will know and it will set your mood that will be beneficial to your loved one. She/he may not know what you did, but will know something happened that they found pleasing. When my wife stroked my short goatee I wriggle my whole body. She got a really big kick out of that. If you want to put a smile on someone's face that you really care about, try that if you dare. If you do, you'll experience a contented gladness that will envelope the room you both occupy. Glad is a bridge word between ok and wow! You will be glad to help someone else's day a tad, or maybe two tads better than great!

Use this word everyday for a week. Check yourself below.						
Sun	M	T	W	T	F	Sat

Better Words For Better Living

> **Great:** adjective: huge, grand, famous, talented, skillful, impressive, remarkable
>
> *Thomas Jefferson was truly a great man.*

One of my favorite *great* men was Thomas Jefferson. As one of the founding fathers of the United States, he accomplished many remarkable feats to make this the great country where we now live.

Occasionally when I give one of my workshops or seminars I will ask everyone to stand and yell "I FEEL GREAT." That certainly sets the mood and in many instances wakes folks up. It is a great icebreaker

When people ask me how I'm doing, I will either say 'GREAT' or I am two tads above fantastic. You see people like people who verbalize that they are feeling good. Suppose you had a challenging day or are not looking forward to a particular task. Well, tell yourself and everyone around you that you are doing great. It will help you, honest, it works.

A smile and a cheerful "I am feeling great" will help you throughout the day and well into the evening. Try it. It's worth the effort.

What makes you feel great? Write down all the triggers that make you feel great, from the past, present or that might be in the future. Some good examples include; a song, a poem, a movie and or a person. Then write down what and why those items made you feel so remarkable. Did you or do you have a great car, a great friend or a song that made you feel great?

I know it is challenging to always feel great, but if you force yourself to smile or even whistle or hum one of those favorite tunes, it will change your demeanor and people will notice the difference. But better yet, they'll want to be around you and they'll more likely be willing to cooperate with you in almost every way.

Do you remember what Cassius Clay/Mohammad Ali always said? "I am the greatest." Arguably, he was the greatest fighter in the ring. Of course, he had a punch that backed him up. He announced he was going to win the battle and in what round!

There are many great men and women in history and a lot of books have been written about them. One of the greatest women in modern times once said when asked; "Will you march against war?" She answered, "No but I will march for peace." Her name, is Mother Theresa.

She did great things every day of her long life, helping the severely afflicted, comforting them with the "milk of human kindness." This humble but revered champion of the forgotten and abandoned is truly great!

Use this word everyday for a week. Check yourself below.						
Sun	M	T	W	T	F	Sat

Better Words For Better Living

> **Happy:** adjective: feeling of joy, contentment, or a pleasureable nature
>
> *When I visited with my sister over the Thanksgiving holidays it was a most pleasing experience and they were very happy to extend their "southern hospitality."*

Have you ever seen a baby happy? If you want a happiness pill, find a happy baby. Spend a little time with a happy baby and I guarantee your mood will be a lot better than when you walked into the room. There's a baby who never fails to make my wife and me happy. Her name is Charlotte and she's the granddaughter of one of our best friends. Charlotte is a delightfully happy baby, always smiling and giggling. At two years old, she's a great soccer player as well.

Happiness seems to come easily to some folks. Others, just have to work at it a little harder. One of my favorite people games is to help transform the mood and attitude of a bleak conversation by subtly interjecting a happy thought followed up with another that's a little more obvious. That's because folks sometime have a difficult time realizing that it's better to be happy than not. Oh, I know you can't be happy all the time, but you can try!

Did you know that most people are as happy as they make up their mind to be! I didn't make that up. A bearded gentleman on every five-dollar bill said it more than a little while ago. For those who know little about Abraham Lincoln, our 16th President, he had all the excuses in the world to be unhappy, but was happy nevertheless. That was one of his many outstanding tattributes that helped him get elected.

If you read his biography you will be astonished and impressed at how hard he worked overcoming adversities. Of course, there are hundreds maybe thousands of famous people who, by virtue of having a happy outlook, experienced a positive attitude adjustment.

"A Christmas Carol," one of Charles Dickens's most famous novels, illustrates the power of being happy loud and clear. In the tale, Scrooge, a miserly old man is visited by the ghosts of Christmas past, present and future, which turns out to be the most devastating of all. Fortunately for him he changed his attitude from a sad old man to a happier one. Like Scrooge, all of us can benefit by changing our attitudes to be as happy as we want to be.

If you want a good start to being happy, try limiting your news watching or reading! Most of it, about 80%, is downright depressing! So, begin your day by reading a good personal development book. Thousands of excellent ones are available in books stores, libraries and on the Internet. Those books will help you become happier, but for a real kick-start to happiness, find a happy baby.

Use this word everyday for a week. Check yourself below.						
Sun	M	T	W	T	F	Sat

Better Words For Better Living

> **Helping:** verb, adverb: serving, selection, portion
>
> *When we volunteer at a local hospice or soup kitchen, we are helping those who do not presently have the ability to help themselves.*

How you choose to help is the key to how happy you feel. You can help those who need help, or you can serve yourself. What is that about? Is it about you or is it about those you helping? This is a very personal question that you need to address when deciding to help others.

From time to time, I give talks and lectures at various organizations. I also do some volunteering and find it very rewarding. It makes me feel good. I like to store those "good feelings" in my imaginary "storage bag" that's always with me so I can draw from it when things get difficult, as you know they will. It keeps me balanced with my other bag, which contains mostly garbage.

At one event, one of the attendees gave me a very pointed retort when I told them about how I felt. He said "Are you going for the people you are helping or are you going for yourself?" I don't often get flustered, but I did briefly. I answered him truthfully. The answer was yes and yes. As long as you are helping people and they do not feel you're just being charitable, they will respect you. I enjoy helping others. When they respond favorably, they're actually helping me. Get it? He gave me a puzzled look, and may have had to reflect a bit before he got it! For the record, he was a self-proclaimed agnostic… hmmmm. Could that account for his look?

If I know anything, it's that there's a higher power and that He put us here to help our brothers and sisters. He also gave us the option to choose how we feel and how we help others to feel. I also know that when I help others feel good, I feel good. It doesn't necessarily make me better than others, but it does help me be do better in all that I do.

Use this word everyday for a week. Check yourself below.						
Sun	M	T	W	T	F	Sat

Better Words For Better Living

> **Indicate:** verb: specify, reveal, show, make known, designate
>
> *Someone in authority may indicate that you are better suited than someone else to carry out an assignment.*

I like the word "indicate." It's stronger than imply but not as forceful as a demand or command. To get your point across to someone you may indicate an opinion. Let them talk and you listen! This is one way I have of learning. Has anyone indicated to you, either verbally or non-verbally that you may have "stepped over the line?" That happened to me with both of my wives. Do you think they may have something there, or did I just marry two of a kind?

I remember once in my youth, I had a summer job at the Philadelphia Credit Bureau doing research. I had an incredible crush on an older woman. She was all of 19 and I a mere 16 ½. Hey that ½ meant a lot when you're almost grown. I was so struck by her, I could hardly work on the job. To top it all off, she was a very kind and super nice person and willing to help anyone. She had helped me on many occasions as I was learning what to do. The attention she paid to me was of course an indication that she was madly in love with me, especially when she smiled. That smile always made my knees tremble. I was blissfully infatuated.

Bill Becker

Soon enough, two barrels blasted out me of my fantasy world. One day, as I was entering the building to our offices, I saw her with another boy, who I thought was rather ugly. I saw her kiss him and wave goodbye. Boom. The first barrel hit me hard!

She and I took the same elevator to the 11th floor. My mind raced to make up a story as to who he might be. Was he a brother or worse, an old boy friend? Just as I convinced myself into believing one of these imagined conclusions, the women in the elevator started giggling and squealing.

Then the second barrel hit me! The love of my life had gotten engaged the night before! I was sick, I mean really sick! I went up to my boss immediately to ask for the day off. After a visit to the men's room. I went home and stayed out for two more days just moaning. Well the summer ended and she got married and I never saw her again. If by some chance or other this person is reading this now, she'll know my story concerning an indication how one of the best summers I ever had came and went.

Use this word everyday for a week. Check yourself below.						
Sun	M	T	W	T	F	Sat

Better Words For Better Living

> **Initiate:** verb: begin, open, commence, make the first move, get started
>
> *To initiate strategic thinking you must begin with a well thought out plan of action.*

Overcoming inertia requires making the first move. Often, personal emotional issues stop us from getting started. But once started, we must continue stoking the flames of passion, because deeply felt personal passion, initiates action.

Often when writing, I just sit there and "think." That's really a way to start. Frequently, "it" will come to me. "It" could be an idea for a book, or just an idea for making peoples' lives better or any number of things. Once I make a plan on how to get started, I become the beneficiary of this process.

When I begin any project, I use my Goal Action Sheets (GAS) because they work. Using them stimulates and inspires me to move forward. But it's not enough to write down your goals and action steps. You must implement those steps to achieve your goals. In my book "Discovering the Power Within," I utilize my **PIFT** system — **Plan, Implement, Follow Through.** It always works as long as I am persistent in making the plan work.

Do you have a passion? I am sure you do if you just think about it long enough. Recently, at one of my two-hour seminars, I asked, "What is your why?" One of the attendees said he would like to go fishing in Alaska. "Fine," I said. "How are you going to initiate your plan?" He was reluctant to answer. However, after the seminar he shared with me and the class that he now knew what he wanted to do and it was much bigger than fishing in Alaska. It was helping others who wanted to visit Alaska but could not afford the trip. Even though he was in poor health, he was really excited when he left the seminar and could hardly wait to initiate his plan.

Initiate change in YOUR life right now. Your goals are within your grasp, if you use the power of your mind and your power from within. Do it now, you'll be amazed.

Use this word everyday for a week. Check yourself below.						
Sun	M	T	W	T	F	Sat

Better Words For Better Living

> **Join:** verb: link, fix, sign up, unite, connect, bond, become a member, fasten together
>
> *Some people have yet to join human kind because of their prejudices.*

Join means different things to different people. Personally, I like joining things like network groups, golf clubs, nonprofits. The list could go on and on. But I like the word best when it represents a meeting of the minds on a particular subject or idea.

When I was a young kid, I joined several boys clubs, which included YMCA's. Generally, I had a grand time. I am a people person and like people. But, a mentor was told me, "There were only about nine or ten really nasty people in the world, and they move around a lot." And yes, I have met one or two, but of course they were not on my top favorite people list. However, over the years, I've found no matter who you meet, if you treat people with courtesy and respect, you will most likely get along.

Joining network groups is perhaps one of my favorite things. I've found that most people join various groups to expand their own network. I believe that means there's something in it for everybody. My creed tells me I need to make every attempt to sincerely reach out to people and help them first, without any expectations of getting any thing in return. For me, it's a become a proven way of making new friends and business associates. There are many of different types of networking groups around. Not all of them exist for business reasons. You can fine one like a Chess Club, just for fun.

Early in my first marriage, before any of my 3 children were born, I joined a chess club where I worked. I actually became quite adept at playing. That's because I would always ask to be pitted against the best chess player. My Dad taught me this when he taught me how to play chess. He said, "If you want to get really good at anything, you must get knocked down many times before you become the knocker!"

My wife was 9 plus months pregnant when I had entered a chess tournament. The matches were held about a half hour from our apartment. You can probably guess what happened! Yep, she called the club just as I was on a roll making some winning moves. I rushed home to find her in the shower singing

When she came out and got dressed, she started watching TV, even though she was having labor pains about every six minutes. The movie she was watching was an oldie called "Marjorie Morningstar" and she decided she wanted to see it to the end.

All the signs indicated that she was just about ready. I knew I had to initiate what I thought was a real emergency action. "Let's go to the hospital

Better Words For Better Living

NOW," I yelled.

She got up and then sat right back down. She said, "I have decided that I am not going to do this," (have the baby that is).

I told her she didn't have much choice. I'm no doctor but even I could see it was time to get moving. So I bundled her up and off we went.

She delivered a beautiful baby girl and everything tuned out great. My "queen of angels," Regina Angelique, was and still is the light of my life. Every day thereafter, I join my hands together in prayer to thank our God for this special gift.

Use this word everyday for a week. Check yourself below.							
Sun	M	T	W	T	F	Sat

> **Joy:** noun: delight, thrill, bliss, elation, pleasure, ecstasy, happiness
>
> *My children and my grandchildren are the great joy in my life!*

Joy is a noun, but it's also an incredibly grand feeling of happiness impossible to describe. Have you experienced joy? Of course you have, just as I have. But have you ever really deeply appreciated delight in your life? The busy world tends to distract us from actually seeing the many joy producing experiences that surround us daily.

I have a favorite saying, "Follow Your Bliss!" I discovered it while watching a PBS documentary about Joseph Campbell. He was a American writer and scholar, most well known for his work in mythology and comparative religion. It was Campbell who coined that phrase and it became his philosophy. To me, Campbell manifested bliss in everything he did. You might say that he was an Olympic Gold Medalist in spiritual gymnastics.

There is very little difference between spiritual and physical gymnastics. That's because they are bound together by one idea, and that's "discipline." When you combine these ideas they really enhance the game of life. Perhaps the Martial Arts are a good example of this concept. The Martial Arts combine the spiritual and physical with discipline while striving to obtain the highest level of achievement, getting a black belt.

So what does it take for us to become a "black belt" in Joy? It takes the discipline to start more closely observing daily life and deriving more joy from the little things like a child's happy smile. There are many things that can bring us joy such as a job well done, accomplishments of our loved ones, a victory in the throes of defeat, an hour well lived, especially one where we are helping others without reward. The list is endless if you're constantly on the lookout for those joy filled moments.

We must all be seekers of joy and providers of joy as well, because creating joy is just as important as witnessing it and experiencing it. Doing so will double or triple your joy. Follow your bliss each and every day and your bounty will be unending.

Use this word everyday for a week. Check yourself below.							
Sun	M	T	W	T	F	Sat

> **Kind:** noun: nice, compassionate, caring, considerate, gentle, benevolent, thoughtful
>
> *To be kind and compassionate to those less fortunate than us is a sign of integrity and character.*

Being kind to animals, children and the elderly is an admirable trait. But being kind to oneself is a life worth living. It's easy for some people. Others have to work at it until it becomes automatic.

We should extend kindness because it makes us feel better to be kind and to help others. I know some folks are thinking, "That is a selfish thought." Well guess what, being selfish to be kind is not a bad thing! I know the gruffest people who are kind and sympathetic to everyone except themselves. That tells you something about them. If they were kind and considerate in their minds, spirit and emotions, they would not be considered gruff.

I borrowed the idea of "how can we help others before helping ourselves," from Dale Carnegie's most famous book, "How to Win Friends and Influence People." This concept works well in all aspects of our lives but it's especially helpful in business.

We all have to do some sort of networking. So whenever I network, I follow my network rule; I always put new people I meet first by asking, "How I can I help to you grow your business?" This leads

Better Words For Better Living

into a conversation about their business first, not mine. Be clear. I tell them when we first meet we're here to help each other. This works in personal situations as well. Talk about them first, not yourself!

Do you remember when you fell in love? Chances are everything was wonderful. Then, the romance may have cooled off a bit. Not because the chemistry was gone, but more likely because you saw some possible character flaws that you found displeasing. To rekindle the flame of love will take work. Yes, I did say that nasty four letter word, WORK! You need to work on yourself to once again become the person your love knew. Love is not a battleground of winners and losers. Being kind is a wonderful middle ground.

Remember, being kind is NOT a sign of weakness. It shows you're strong. Understanding everything about the circumstances, whether difficult or easy, is one of the first steps. It's about considering someone else first. I think being unselfish is another term for being kind. Today, be kind to those who may not deserve it. Remember, you deserve a little kindness too.

Use this word everyday for a week. Check yourself below.							
Sun	M	T	W	T	F	Sat	

Bill Becker

> **Kiss:** noun, verb: smooch, affectionate touch with the lips
>
> *There are many types and styles of kisses, but the best kiss is from a loved one.*

I am not sure what the kiss of death is, but I'm sure what the kiss of life is. When you are in love and you cannot get enough kissing and I'm sure anyone who has been in love knows all about the kiss of life.

Occasionally, I visit Jackson, my wife's grandson. His kiss is especially wonderful, as only a baby's kiss can be. He opens his mouth wide and boom, plants a big smacker, in your eye, nose or wherever. A kiss like his is one of life's little joys, to be remembered and cherished.

Jackson was a preemie! He and his mother, Julie, almost didn't make into the world. His grandmother, my wife Eleanor, strongly believed that the power of our prayers, along with prayers of thousands of others, via electronic media, saved them. Eleanor kisses Jackson at least a dozen times whenever she visits with him, and that is often.

I'm a tad jealous of families that kiss and hug when meeting and leaving. Mine was not like that. But I am instilling that with my daughter and my wife, Eleanor is helping with my sons and certainly our grandsons. I have six, she has two. We've

Better Words For Better Living

become a kissy, huggy family. For us, a kiss is an expression of love, affection and closeness.

When I was ten, I was smitten with a little raven haired Jewish girl my age. My friends told me she was Jewish even though I didn't know or care what that meant. All I cared about was that she was pretty and liked me. We talked and giggled and smiled at each other during class. I wanted to get close to her but wasn't totally sure of how to do that.

In my imagination, I conjured up the hero in the Cowboy movies I'd seen at ten cent Saturday matinees. The cowboy got a kiss for saving the girl from some sort of peril. But Barbara Weinberg's life is no danger that I could rescue her from. So I just came out and said "I love you and would you give me a kiss?"

She had been eating a carrot at the time. As in most emotional situations in life, my timing wasn't well thought out. Barbara looked at me and kissed the carrot and said, "now you kiss the carrot and that is your kiss." Of course I did and that was my first kiss. I'll never forget that fantastic moment. So go ahead. Kiss someone today and every day — not just anyone, but someone you care for and respect.

Use this word everyday for a week. Check yourself below.							
Sun	M	T	W	T	F	Sat

> **Laugh:** noun, verb: express amusement, giggle, snicker, and chuckle.
>
> *People sometimes laugh at the most ridiculous actions of others.*

I know that God has a sense of humor because I've born the brunt of it. I contend that if we can laugh at ourselves it's really God. One memorable example involved driving to the New Jersey shore of the Atlantic. I made 4 wrong turns in a row and then another. I pulled over and smacked myself on the forehead so hard that I nearly passed out.

As I came to my senses and laughed at myself, I noticed my wife was also laughing. It's amusing when someone else is laughing because laughing can be contiguous.

Many years ago, while on a short flight from New York to Philadelphia in an 8 passenger prop plane, I noticed a young man who was visibly uncomfortable about flying. Even though his companion tried to assure him flying was quite safe, he remained unconvinced. Belted in, we took off. As we ascended, the young man started laughing nervously. Soon, I also was laughing. All the passengers joined in, including a grumpy looking gentlemen. The laughter lasted the entire 26 minute flight. As we departed, the flight attendant thanked the young man for keeping everyone happy.

Better Words For Better Living

My Father was a kindly man. He loved animals. When I was around 15, he found a wounded pigeon in our back yard. He took the pigeon in and built a cage for it and kept it in our basement. He nursed that pigeon like it was a baby. My mother was not too keen on the idea. To her, pigeons were flying rats carrying all kinds of bugs. But my father kept it the entire winter. He was quite proud and very attached to the bird. One day when I came home, my mother was laughing so hard I thought she'd wet herself. I said, "Mom what's so funny?" She said, your father put the bird cage in the backyard this morning before he left for work. I just went outside to hang some clothes up and all that was in the cage were feathers." Well mom, I'm sure God forgave you for laughing, but I bet my father hasn't." Sometimes we to tend to laugh at someone else's misfortune.

Norman Cousins was diagnosed with terminal cancer. He decided to take a cruise, stay in his state room and watch funny movies of the Three Stooges, Laurel and Hardy, Abbot and Costello and other greats. He came home cured and wrote a book about his experience. This also has been medically proven with a number of similar cases.

Be sure to laugh this week it is good for the soul.

Use this word everyday for a week. Check yourself below.						
Sun	M	T	W	T	F	Sat

Bill Becker

> **Love:** noun, verb: worship, adore, care for, be very fond of, feel affection for, tenderness, fancy, passionate about
>
> *The love of another person is a blissful experience when reciprocated in a like manner and in a healthy behavior.*

I'm not going to attempt to outdo any of the great writers such as Shakespeare or Kahil Gibran, who so eloquently spoke of love, focus on the "love of humanity." It seems lacking in many modern societies. Yet, interpreting the idea of love of humanity can be a daunting task.

Throughout history, many great people illustrated its meaning in everyday life. The truth is, most were not famous at all. They just believe and work tirelessly at loving and serving humanity. We see them but don't always recognize them. Some call them "do gooders."

Well I say here's three cheers for the "do gooders." There are far too few of them. They don't go about shouting "here I am." No, they quietly work tirelessly, without fanfare, helping others who cannot or won't help themselves in life's challenging circumstances.

One such person with whom I am associated wants to remain anonymous and I respect his wish. His deeds are synonymous with love of mankind especially in the areas of drug, alcohol and other types of addictions. I was in his company just before going on retreat to Weston Priory to work on this book.

Better Words For Better Living

He got a call from a new client who was clearly distressed. I was in ear shot of the conversation waiting for him to finish. Though I couldn't hear all the details, I waited patiently until he finished explaining to her that he would assign her a counselor.

He always answers his cell phone so I asked him why doesn't he get someone else to handle his calls. He is extremely popular giving speeches on spirituality and other subjects such as co-dependency. His response was that there is always someone every day that needs to have understanding.

As Director and Founder of a busy organization, you might run into him with a plunger going to fix a toilet. Humility best describes him. He's my hero because he depicts the kind of love for humankind that I aspire to. Every day I strive to do things better than I did the day before. I have heart shaped buttons I had made over twenty years ago. Occasionally, I give them out at my self improvement seminars. Maybe we'll meet at one of my programs someday.

To sum up the word love, it's an experience of bliss, an extension of God's love, which is for all humanity. We all need love and must emulate and follow His son's path.

Use this word everyday for a week. Check yourself below.						
Sun	M	T	W	T	F	Sat

Bill Becker

> **More:** adjective: other, extra, further, additional, in addition to, supplementary
>
> *May I have some more cherry pie please?*

My late spiritual advisor, Sister Charity Kohl, wrote me just a few days before she passed away, "To have more is what and what is more?" I haven't thought about that scribbled passage for many years until now, as I write about the word more.

Question; do we need more? And if so, then more of what? Are we speaking of material "things" or pleasures? How many cars can you drive at once Mr. Leno? How many buildings can you conduct business in Mr. Trump?

Many years ago, one of the most popular songs told us that what we need more of was "Love, Love, Love."

The vast majority of Americans not only has much more than the majority of the world's people but we also give more than virtually any other country in world. As the Good Book says, "To those that have more, more shall be given."

There is no doubt it means many different things to many people. My take is really quite simple — the way to increase your wealth is to increase the wealth of others. You do this by giving and giving and then giving more.

Better Words For Better Living

If you were to track the rich and the super rich, you'll find that their giving habits are more than just tithing ten percent. There are other ways of giving. My wife Eleanor gave more with her time. She volunteered every Wednesday evening at the Food Pantry in Camden, New Jersey, which is often referred to as "the most dangerous city in the USA." Barely five tall, I really worried about her safety until I was found out two burly men escorted her to and from her car.

Don't let her size fool you. She was one tough little "Sigiy," not to be messed with. I affectionately called her that because of her Sicilian descent. Another clue to how tough she was is the fact that she slept on the door side of our bed, *with a knife and a hammer* on her night table. I always felt very safe at her side knowing that if a robber got past her, he would be in really bad shape if he got to me..ha ha. So when it came to toughness she certainly was tougher than the average person.

So, what does "more" mean to you? What is your understanding? If there's one thing I know it's that when you give more, you'll ultimately get more - a whole lot more.

Use this word everyday for a week. Check yourself below.							
Sun	M	T	W	T	F	Sat

> **Muster:** verb: assemble, meet, rally, get together, marshal, aggregate
>
> *One of the best ways to muster support for an idea is obtain a consensus to your side, this is true leadership.*

Whether you like his politics or not, to me, President Ronald Reagan represented a true American hero. He resolved the Iranian hostages crisis, condemned communism and told the leader of the Soviet Union, Mr. Gorbochev, "Take down this wall," which divided the city since WW ll. Reagan's comment on the Wall was a mustering of national and international support for all who hunger for freedom!

Little children are great at mustering support for what they want. First, they'll go to one parent and ask, "Can I have a bicycle?" Most likely the parent will say, "If it is ok with your father (or mother) then it is OK with me." So the next step for mustering support is to go to the other parent and say, "Mom (or dad) said it would be ok to get a bicycle if it's OK with you." I know it seems to easy but mustering support for an idea such as Freedom, or a material object like a bicycle, requires a thought process for accomplishing a definite purpose.

Purpose is energizing. It's why you enthusiastically muster the strength and passion to achieve. It's why you muster help when you need. It's why you keep going. It's why you don't quit.

Better Words For Better Living

I remember the time when I ran for a local political office in my Ward in Philadelphia. I encountered many obstacles. To begin with, I was running against a well-known political name whose first cousin was the former Mayor. And my opponent used this leverage to its fullest extent because the Mayor was very popular. My opponent had a charismatic Kennedy-like image that he used to his advantage. So, how was I going to obtain the majority of the 60 votes to win the position?

He was far ahead in the vote count just days before election but wanted to make it a landslide. I needed for him to stumble over his own arrogance, which he did. His campaign pitch promised jobs. But this promise was his big mistake. He threatened dismissal of those who had jobs unless they would vote for him. In those days, this was the typical campaign. But as it definitely not my style, how would I win? I needed some powerful person to muster some serious support for me.

How about the Mayor in office? But he stayed on the sidelines, saying, "May the best person." One of my supporters came to me crying, afraid that her husband was going to be dredging the Delaware River as a policemen instead of the important police position he presently had.

Since the present mayor was the former Police Commissioner I thought that he would have taken this threat as a personal affront to one of his loyal troops while he was the commissioner.

When I spoke on this person's behalf, he mustered all his people to help me. He personally phoned all the people who were going to vote in that Ward election and asked them to vote for me. Done deal! I was almost elected unanimously, 59 to 1. Guess who that one was?

Yes, you can call it luck or providence or whatever you like. Many people in my life have called me lucky for the things I have accomplished, but you know, the harder I work and the more I keep it positive, the luckier I get. That's why I have managed to muster many of the better things in life.

Use this word everyday for a week. Check yourself below.						
Sun	M	T	W	T	F	Sat

Better Words For Better Living

> **Necessary:** adjective: indispensable, vital, needed, required, essential, basic, obligatory
>
> *One of the necessary elements for humankind to live in harmony is to treat each other with heartfelt kindness.*

Water, food and air are the necessary elements to sustain life of the physical body, but isn't the mind a key part of the body?

The late Zig Ziglar, was a long time friend and mentor. He believed that in order to be a success in anything, you had to help other people obtain what they want or need first, and if you continue to do that, you'll surely succeed. His most famous saying was, "Garbage in garbage out!" Of course this is a metaphor for whatever you put in your mind will either come out as garbage or wisdom. And when wisdom comes out, you'll succeed.

Wisdom is always at your calling. For me, seeking wisdom is a matter of asking my maker. Seems simple, but most of life's pleasantries are simple to attain though they may be difficult to understand. The instruction book to understanding is the Bible. While other religions have their version of the Bible, the bottom line it is each version contains wisdom as long as it includes the necessary element of love.

Loving one another is the key that opens all doors to wisdom and success. We all are instilled with this wisdom. Unfortunately, most people completely ignore it or worse, abuse it. I too have fallen into this category and paid a high price. If you were to think this through you'll readily admit to the same. Do you remember your parents telling you to always look both ways when crossing a street? This idea was instilled in all of us; a piece of wisdom passed down through many generations.

So at the ripe cocky age of 23, I was crossed a very wide street in Philadelphia. Instead of looking in both directions, I only looked at one. When I got to the middle, a very large passenger bus was barreling down the other side coming right across my path. As I was to about to step out of the way (the way I looked) there was another bus also coming right at me. No time to run. There was nothing to do but say some quick prayers. The prayers worked! The buses missed me with just a few inches, on either side of my body. My endorphins kicked in after being sandwiched between those two behemoths of modern travel. I walked quickly to the closest church and made some very long and devout thanks to our Lord.

You see, when we ignore wisdom we suffer a great deal and our lives can get impacted from something as simple as looking both ways when crossing a street. I hope you got the point of this true story. Maybe you've experienced something similar. If you didn't, grab this piece of wisdom then watch out for that bus. It may come sooner than you think, especially when you're not really looking for it.

Better Words For Better Living

To my way of thinking, there's a fourth element necessary for life. It's called wisdom and all of us need to make it an essential part of our lives.

Use this word everyday for a week. Check yourself below.						
Sun	M	T	W	T	F	Sat

Bill Becker

> **Nice:** adjective: Polite, fine, good, pleasant, kind
>
> *When someone does a god deed for someone in need it is said he/she has done a nice thing to help that person.*

I like this word. I think it's nice, but a tad weak. It's the sort of general word that gets us off the hook. For a wordsmith, nice is adequate. But a truly skilled wordsmith would combine nice with other words both before and after. You have heard the term if someone who threw a strike in bowling or defeated a top tennis player in a fiercely fought tennis match. It would be; a really nice strike, really or a very nice stroke you had today, really. Ok, I am reaching, but you get the gist!

I would prefer you complimented someone and said, "What a really nice thing you did for that elderly person crossing the street" That is if you had not tripped him accidently and he fell but was not hurt. You can say the Good Samaritan did an exceptionally nice thing by helping the man who was robbed. That's much better than nice of course! Doing nice things for our fellow human beings makes us feel better.

When we do nice things, some chemicals in our brains are released and make us feel better. Some people are addicted to being nice and that is good. All of us should be addicted to nice. As someone

Better Words For Better Living

once said, "Let's treat everyone as if it were Christmas!" Aren't we all nice at Christmas? Well, most of us anyway. Even Mr. Scrooge ended up being nice.

A nice gesture would be to give a homeless person something to eat. In fact, if you worked or lived in area where there were homeless people, feeding one of them would be a really nice act. The other person who occasionally comes out of hiding in you may claim that they are not homeless, just lazy and drunk.

Now that's the time for you to exclaim, "bah humbug," and in addition to the food, give the person a big Christmas smile even though it might only be Thursday!

On the other hand, the little devil inside might say you are weak for being nice. Here's what I say to that. In my view, Ronald Reagan was one of our nicest Presidents. Was he weak? I think not. He demanded that Russia tear down the Berlin wall and they did. I bet he said, "Thank you Mr. Gorbochev, that was a really nice thing you did."

Use this word everyday for a week. Check yourself below.							
Sun	M	T	W	T	F	Sat	

> **Outstanding:** adjective: great, terrific, marvelous, superior, exceptional, excellent, stupendous
>
> *Mozart and Schubert have produced many outstanding arias and operas.*

This is one of my favorite words strong enough to stand on its own. An outstanding achiever is one who produces more, far more. High achievers share their abundance with others. There are those that surpass the "Biblical ten percent" of give with fifty percent or more of what they earn.

One the most outstanding people of the 20th century was Carnegie, the owner of US Steel and many more companies. His vow and the fulfillment of that vow to give away ninety percent of what he had, was completed by the time of his death, in his nineties. Wow. Yes sir. He gave away ninety percent of what he had. He did not want nor seek fame for what he accomplished.

Think about what was your most outstanding achievement? Which one really sticks out? Is it personal, finance, health, education, business or spiritual? Being on earth 70 plus years, for me, my most outstanding achievement is in the spiritual realm. I work on it daily. To me, that is an important and major outstanding accomplishment in my life.

There are many other areas that people would

Better Words For Better Living

think were outstanding. When it's time to be called to our maker what will you be able to say is your most outstanding accomplishment? These are profound questions that only you can answer for yourself.

You don't have to have the fame or recognition of an Albert Scweitzer, Billy Graham, Ben Franklin, Franz Schubert or an Andrew Carnegie. You just have to be you and leave this world a little better than when you entered. Time is short. Lost time is irretrievable. Treat every day as if you will be accountable to the Big Guy. You may not remember the Ten Commandments but if you just keep the first two the rest fall in line.

Will you forgive those nasty people who did wrong by you? Will you embrace and love them? Only you can make it happen, so get to work. It will take lots of emotional work, but the ultimate payoff is incredible both here and now and elsewhere. Forget about your shortcomings and weaknesses. Work to improve on your strengths and use them to help those less fortunate because that is who you really are. Begin right now — this hour, this minute.

Use this word everyday for a week. Check yourself below.						
Sun	M	T	W	T	F	Sat

Bill Becker

> **Okay:** adjective: acceptable, tolerable, satisfactory, agree to, all right and approve
>
> *Is it okay to help someone less fortunate than you?*

I have a lot of favorite words and okay is one of them. It is also my wife's grandson, Jackson's favorite word. He is only two and uses it a lot especially when he is unsure or frightened. To me, he's starting out more than okay. He knows that some positive self-talk helps regardless of his fear. Think about what we can learn from many two year olds.

My spiritual advisor for many years, the late Sister Charity Kohn, was a highly educated expert in child behavior. She was the founder of CORA services (Check it out on Google). She said the most formative ages for humans are from 2-7. Keep that in mind when you are around children in that age group.

Recently, I was in the company of 7 of them. It was a party for a one year old. Of course all the friends' family of the parents was there with their 2-7 year olds.

I just sat back and, yes entirely enjoyed the commotion and the funny moments. They were extremely entertaining. Here were our future, business people, mechanics, politicians, law offices and maybe even a President thrown in for good measure.

Better Words For Better Living

This was certainly an okay experience for me. Remember, I'm at the age when I can say to my daughter or grandson, "This one has a stinky bottom - clean it up."

Some may say that is "old school" but that's okay by me. There's a book out called, "I'm OK – You're OK." It's a great title and I read it a while back. Many people think that it always means they approve. I think not. It does depend on the circumstances and the inflection when saying "OK" and also on mood and tone of voice.

Wow, I may be venturing in some heady psyche stuff. I just call it good old common sense, notice the old in there.

Then there's "A-OKAY." It doesn't get better than that unless it is a double A OKAY. You know, it may be a tad silly, but I think it is okay to act silly from time to time. It's kind of nice for someone to ask you if you are okay, but if you're asked too often, it can be annoying. You can have too much okay just like rice pudding (if you like rice pudding) but all and all too much is okay is better than not enough or none.

Everyone knows the universal hand sign for OK is the thumb and finger formed in a circle. But you had better ask if you are in a foreign country, because President Nixon caused a major international issue when he came strutting out of Air Force One and put his common V hand sign which signifies peace in

America but not so in other countries. I just learned something the other day that if you do not extend your hand out to shake it in France that they consider you to be rude and insensitive and respond accordingly.

All these years I thought they were rude and insensitive, but all along it was really me. So we need to have some patience with others who are not familiar with our culture as well.

Use this word everyday for a week. Check yourself below.						
Sun	M	T	W	T	F	Sat

Better Words For Better Living

> **Patience:** noun: endurance, tolerance, fortitude, serenity, non complaining
>
> *We must have patience and understanding when dealing with difficult people to earn their respect.*

We have all heard the phrase; "if we have patience everything will work out." This is an axiom that's been passed down through the years. I believe the older we get it seems the less patience we have. That's because we expect everyone we come in contact with should do his or her "thing" right and in our time frame. This is especially true with our children and adults older than we are.

Certainly Jesus Christ had to endure the disciples. His patience was tested hundreds of times. Likewise, His temptations were also tested. We must have the same patience with our children and others, but especially our children because they just don't know. We think they should, but they don't! You're probably thinking, "Adults must know." After all, they have lived longer than children. But guess what? Some, if not all of them, haven't experienced patience in their upbringing. It's just a lack of training by the adults who also needed training.

The best coaches in any sport are those who have a great deal of patience. They see raw talent but know that they need to teach their players to take their time and focus on their skills and fail many times before getting better.

Babe Ruth holds the record for striking out. One of the reasons was that he was at bat more times than most players. But he knew his skill and waited for a pitch he knew he could hit. Then he slammed the ball.

Golf, now there's a game of patience! If you want to learn patience, play golf. I do and enjoy it even more when I am patient with myself, the weather and other golfers. Regardless of the conditions, if I exercise more patience I will always play a better round.

I recently learned three steps. One, set myself. Two, take a deep breath and wait (patience). Three, swing from my hips. These tiny steps have knocked off 20 strokes from my game. Oh there is one more directly from the movie Caddy Shack. Chevy Chase says, "Be the ball!"

The game of life is virtually the same. Set yourself, take a deep breath (have patience) and swing with all the gusto you have. Be in the game of life and enjoy each day even though it may be a struggle. You have more to learn from your struggles than you do your successes.

Use this word everyday for a week. Check yourself below.							
Sun	M	T	W	T	F	Sat

Better Words For Better Living

> **Play:** verb: engage in some sort of recreation, amuse yourself with or without others, have fun.
>
> *My wife and I will occasionally play a card game, while flying to a destination, to have fun.*

The way I define play is to have fun. While there are other meanings, we use it most in reference to fun, in other words, playfully. Now see there I have played with your thoughts and you are not sure what I said!! That's okay; I was just playing with you.

As long as there is no harm done we can play like that. I enjoy playing all sorts of games. One favorite is where I see if I can steer a negative conversation to a positive one without anyone knowing what I am up to. This is a lot of fun for me, and almost always it helps people feel better. Try it. You'll like it.

My wife and I will sometimes visit a casino in nearby Atlantic City, NJ and play the slots. I like to play craps mostly. One time I went by myself. It was my lucky night and I mean very lucky. I hit the slots for $1,000 twice and went and played craps for nearly two hours. It seemed could not lose. I even increased my bets by a large amount and still ended up a winner. Folks at the tables were wondering whether I was a big time gambler. Sure I was. I went to the casinos every three to four months with a strict $100 limit to spend. So you can imagine how I felt when I was actually betting the $25 tables. Boy was I having fun!

I began to get hungry and asked for dinner voucher from the pit boss. Generally they'll, give you a $20 or $30 voucher depending on how much you bet. They took my casino card and took a long time coming back with the voucher. I guess they thought I would go on a losing streak. Not this time. In fact, I picked up another $500 while they were gone.

The voucher said zero! I was a bit upset and told them I had been betting $25 bets not $5 bets and had gambled for more than 2 hours. They said, "Sir, that zero means you can have anything you want at our finest restaurant free of charge. Wow, I like free. I was so happy I made a remark to the pit boss that I wished my wife were here to enjoy the dinner. He told me the casino would pick her up and bring her to the restaurant. I said we lived in Philadelphia, he said no problem. I called her and told her I was taking her to the finest restaurant in Atlantic City, be ready in one hour.

They picked her up and personally escorted her to our table as I sipped on a wine that cost over $100 a bottle. We had a wonderful dinner and I pocketed the six plus thousand dollars and got out of dodge. Play? Indeed,I did play. Thank you lady luck.

Use this word everyday for a week. Check yourself below.						
Sun	M	T	W	T	F	**Sat**

Better Words For Better Living

> **Quaint:** adjective: charming, old school, attractive, old fashioned, appealing, peculiar, extraordinary.fun.
>
> *You may be able to tell some folks' personalities by their quaint taste in furniture, as it may be old fashioned.*

Some call me quaint, which can be interpreted as old school or peculiar. I own it because that's who I am. It is not a bad thing because again, it's who I am. Wow, "I am," just three little letters than can mean so much. So this begs the question are you who you think you are? Can you say this is "who I am?" You see, many people let others define who they are and wonder why they go around somewhat confused about their personalities, about who they really are.

At that point, many people will try to adopt someone else's personalities. Of course actors and actresses get paid for that and we pay to see them metamorphosed on the big or little screens. So can you say you are? Give this some serious thought because it's your life, not someone else's. It may be OK to adopt good points from others that will strengthen our character.

The Great Savior, Jesus Christ, of the Christian religion, which I regularly practice, knew who he was. In fact, in the New Testament, Jesus does in fact answer the question when queried by Pontius Pilate (Who would crucify him). "Are you King of the

Jews?" He answered by saying, "You say that I am." So we like Jesus can also say I am. But it's up to you to determine who you believe you are.

All of us have heard the term "How quaint that...is." I like to think when I hear or see it's used as being deliciously cute. Sometimes I may refer to a person or a house/home or yes, maybe, even a car. I thought my little Porsche was deliciously cute that is after I dressed him up. He was and hopefully might still be around is as I dubbed him Peter. So Peter Porsche had white fur seat covers a 15 coat silver paint job along with a newly painted dashboard, and to top it off, brand new wheels. Yes quaint or cute and a little weird, kind of like me.

The most interesting thing about Peter was how very expensive it cost to own him. Over the 2 years I owned him, he had gone through several clutches, which cost $700 each time. One day while I had the car being serviced for the clutch of course, the clutch, I noticed two people walking around the Porsche as I was paying the mechanic. A teenager about 18 and an older man were eyeing Peter.

Why I need to replace the clutch so frequently was always a mystery to me. I only took it out on the weekends and was very gentle with shifting gears. In total frustration at having to replace yet another clutch, I a approached them and quickly asked the older man, "Do you want to buy my Porsche?"

He responded, "How much?" Being somewhat

Better Words For Better Living

versed on the art of bargaining because of my real estate investing experience, I said what do you think it is worth. I saw a twinkle in the teenager's eye as I imagined he viewed himself behind the wheel very shortly. The older man said I have ten grand in my pocket and proceeded to show it to me. He asked, "Do you have the pink slip?" Yes I do. I was not too eager to jump at the first offer but was inwardly excited. I only paid 4 thousand but had dumped about 3 thousand into it. I said 10 grand it is. Here's an interesting side note. He offered to flip a coin to do a double or nothing. I thought about it for several seconds and quickly said, "No. Let's make the deal and be done with it." He told me his son was starting college next week and needed transportation and this was perfect.

So I sold my Peter Porsche and know he had gone to a good home. And here's another interesting side note. Many years later, my eldest son Billy told me that when he was 16, he used to push the Porsche out of the driveway at night while I was asleep and jump started it by popping the clutch. At last, the mystery of the burned out clutches was finally solved.

Use this word everyday for a week. Check yourself below.						
Sun	M	T	W	T	F	Sat

Bill Becker

> **Quest:** noun or verb: pursuit, hunt, mission, expedition. search, chase, seek, go after
>
> *The Knights of old always had a quest of seeking the Holy Grail.*

That sentence conjures up many movies I saw as a kid. It still does. After all, aren't we all kids in more mature bodies? Errol Flynn was one of my favorite actors in those movies. He portrayed heroes that were always on a quest of saving treasure from the pirates for king and country or rescuing damsels in distress. From what I have read, he was like that in real life, at least the part about chasing ladies, even those not in distress.

A quest can be a goal, yet most people don't have goals. Stop a total stranger and ask, "What are your goals?" Most people will say, "Gee I don't know. I get up most days and go to work just like everyone else." What are your goals? What is your quest? Not what you wish for, but what is your heartfelt quest. What are you doing each day to continue your quest, of finding what you are searching for?

It's a tough question but most people don't have a plausible answer. They'll just drift along and hope they don't go over the falls. There are many people just like you, who drift until they finally go over the falls. Some survive and go on to become great people, not only to the world but also to their

Better Words For Better Living

families and friends. How about taking some time to write about who you think some of them are. Some of them may be in your own family or circle of friends and acquaintances. Or they may be well known celebrities. But their quest is to be a celebrity to themselves. A bit confusing you might say. You see, the quest is always the act of seeking so you cannot celebrate until you find what you are looking to accomplish.

Many quests are focused on money, the almighty dollar. But you need to understand that is just a way of helping you acquire whatever your quest is. There is nothing wrong with that, as long as helping others, and yes even yourself, is part of your quest. The big question is whether you will actually help others once you have completed your quest. The key is to think about helping others as well as yourself at the beginning of your quest.

What is your quest? To open a hospital, orphanage a school for the handicapped? To earn $90,000 each month so you and your family can live comfortably? Or to get to that perfect weight and become physically fit? My suggestion is that you write out what all of your quests. Choose just one as a major quest and invest time, your most valuable asset into the seeking of that quest.

As you know, time is one commodity you cannot recoup. Once spent, it's gone forever. That's a profound idea, but only if you take it seriously. The person about go over the falls wishes he had more time to change direction and go to shore instead of squandering the most precious asset. So once again, my friend, what is your quest? Ask yourself the following questions each day, upon arising and upon going to bed: What is my quest? What actions have I taken in my most sought after quest?

Use this word everyday for a week. Check yourself below.						
Sun	M	T	W	T	F	Sat

Better Words For Better Living

> **Regard:** verb: observe, watch, view, look at or upon
>
> *It is not a bad thing to have a high regard for those who have high moral values, as long as they have humility and are willing to share their gifts with others*

Regard is mostly used in a positive manner. I have high regard for nearly everyone I come in contact with. This is especially true with close friends. I draw on their strength, not suck it from them because they are willing to share this strength. Some people I come in contact I may not hold in high regard. To those, I'll just say, "thank you for sharing" and move on. I'll send them a love prayer that they will someday have as much high regard for others as they have for themselves. Think about that for a minute. You probably know some folks like that. Perhaps they may even be very close to you.

We must be ourselves and love our selves before we can share our love with others. Yes, I know it's difficult or almost impossible in many situations. As I sit here at my laptop listening to the background chatter of the TV, I write what I believe can be of future help to others. However, the singing Monks of the Weston Priory drown the TV noise. This could be my legacy, this book or other books I have written. It really doesn't matter that much to others who hold my book in not so high regard. But there is always an outside chance that it may help someone long after I have gone. Perhaps it might a year from now or maybe a century from now.

Many people hold me in high regard for the fact that I am one of the main caretakers for my wife, Eleanor, who is suffering from Glioblastoma (Brain cancer). Between her daughter and me, we handle 100% of the duties. This really does not deserve the high regard label because it's what we do for those we love, and as a friend who nursed his invalid wife for 12 years told me at her funeral, "It was a joy to be the caretaker for my wife." I have taken that as my mantra as I care for my wife, Eleanor, during this extremely critical time.

Unfortunately, as most who know me, know that I've fought a similar battle with cancer during my first marriage. My quest is to give Eleanor, my present wife, a reasonable if not blissful quality of life as long as she is with me. On a positive note, Eleanor has been surrounded by love from most of her family and friends who keep contacting and visiting, asking if they can do anything. They bring us goodies. She can eat, oh and does, yes she can eat. However, we have her on an organic macrobiotic diet, which excludes dairy, gluten, and limited sugar.

She still has that great smile. It was one of the hooks that got me attracted to her as well as a profound spiritual oneness she exuded. When I first looked in her eyes, I fell deeply in love with her. I

Better Words For Better Living

hold dear all those hundreds of thousands who are praying for her thanks to the Internet and all those who have put her in their prayer lines.

I have high regard for the doctors and research people who are fervently dedicated to conquering the lurking beast called cancer. When I was a young man, I had heard that one of three would get cancer. I believe it because I am experiencing it again right now. With God's help, I have come to the realization that the human race is the cause of this beast. To this end we must, yes I say we must stop feeding our livestock and vegetation the carcinogens that cause cancer because, doing so, we also consume the same items.

The so-called Blue Countries, such as Tibet, Costa Rica and most parts of India have a very low cancer rate. I have high regard for these countries because they stick to God's laws, which are in their religious teachings and writings.

Use this word everyday for a week. Check yourself below.							
Sun	M	T	W	T	F	Sat

Bill Becker

> **Respect:** noun, verb: reverence, esteem, admire, admiration, thinks highly of, defer to, admire, value, look up
>
> *You will earn respect if you act with integrity and humility in your daily actions.*

Even though respect is a key element in gaining favor with those close to us, or in our business relationships, the word really doesn't gain much respect in today's world. One of my favorite "old school" writers and speakers was a gentleman by the name of Dale Carnegie, not to be confused with Andrew Carnegie, the steel billionaire who gave away 90 percent of his fortune before the age 92. Dale was a philosopher of sorts and the famed author of "How to Win Friends and Influence People."

He was also a billionaire, not in money but something extremely more valuable, social/people skills which are rarely used today. Dale is one of the many whom I respect mainly because of his quest to continue to help people change their lives by finding out what others want. His writings have spawned many books on self-development.

You know, back in the day (we old school folks like to use that term), respect was learned from our elders like a grandparent or aunt or uncle. It seems that today parenting isn't so much into teaching respect. As a result, children have little interest and

Better Words For Better Living

probably won't pass the idea on.

So what can you do about it? The answer is you, we, all of us. By showing respect to each other and to children, we let others know that when it comes to getting along, respect is magic. Look for opportunities to give respect to your children and all children as well. Here's how to do it.

Common courtesy and respect are close cousins even though common courtesy is becoming less common today. So let's go back in time, oh let's examine PBS's best watched series, "Downton Abby." The family is always respectful toward each other. Even when one family member is upset with another, they are always very polite. Check it out and you'll see what I mean.

Is there a polite way of telling someone off? You bet there is. First write out in detail what you are going to tell them. Include everything, bad words and all. Then read it to yourself loudly and start to laugh. Yes, I said laugh. Ninety percent of the time you won't take action, and if you do it will be almost whimsical. Now here comes the important part; teach this strategy to your children or grandchildren. You'll get that ball rolling again so people will not only understand respect but will begin to start using this valuable skill of influencing people. But most of all, you're training yourself, as well as future generations.

Here's a simple truth. The more you give respect,

the more you'll get respect. Once you do, you'll start to notice many positive changes. Try it, I guarantee you will like it.

In fact, play a little game with yourself and others. It doesn't cost a thing, but the returns are enormous. Asians have a great deal of respect for their elders and are almost always polite. We Americans should take a hard look at their culture after all they are 5,000 years ahead of us.

Shaking hands is a form of respect if we extend ours first. Many French people don't hold us in high regard because they believe that we show them very little respect. Once while I was in Paris, a Frenchman told me that if Americans would just show some respect for their language by attempting to use it, they would have much more respect for us. Think about that. Don't we feel the same way when someone from another country at least tries to communicate to us in English? Respect. It goes a long way.

Use this word everyday for a week. Check yourself below.						
Sun	M	T	W	T	F	Sat

Better Words For Better Living

> **Smile:** noun, verb: beam, grin, a sing of favor, a pleasant expression, a pleasant appearance
>
> *My daughter, Regina's, face lit up with a warm and friendly smile when I arrived at her home to take her to see the Phillies play baseball.*

Smile is one of my challenging words. Here's why. When I'm deep in thought. I actually look like I am frowning. Friends have told me quite candidly, that I looked like I was angry with them and my next class should be "Anger Management." I am, however, smiling on the inside. Most likely, I'm really not concentrating on smiling. We all need to get in the habit of smiling more whenever we're in contact with people while on the job or with friends and family.

What does the word *smile mean to you*? There are different types of smiles such as; the serene smile, the saccharine smile, the happy smile, and many more. Some people seem to have a permanent smile, while others a permanent frown. Smiling almost forces you into a good mood. For me, babies' smiles are the very best. Think about that for a minute! Even just thinking about a smiling baby can give you a warm and fuzzy feeling.

How about a smile from young lady or man? Some smiles can be almost hot, depending on where they lead. Smile and fun seem to go together like peanut butter and jelly and linking smile with fun can give your life a powerful boost on a daily basis.

Often, we get lost in our thoughts, which are not always positive. When this happens, we're bombarded by negativity. As the song says, "smile," even though it may be difficult. A smile will put pep in your step and change your outlook, even if it's only momentary. Smiles can become habit forming. Feeling good is habit forming. The more you smile the better you feel.

Would you share a story with me about how a smile changed your mood? I'd love to hear from you and just maybe reward you for that story. Send it via email to **Bill@areii.com** and put "I want to share a smile story with you" in the subject line.

Here are a few short "smile" stories that had a positive emotional impact on me that I'd like to share with you.

There I was driving about 7:30 A.M. not thinking about anything in particular. I stopped at a "Go Light" in my neighborhood and standing on the corner was a young lady obviously waiting for a bus. As I pulled away, she looked at me with a very warm, almost intoxicating gaze. Then she suddenly beamed a beautiful toothy smile. I almost wanted to go back and ask her what she had for breakfast because she obviously was feeling really happy. Her smile stayed with me for a week. I never saw her again but even though it's been over 30 years; her radiant smile still has a positive effect on me.

Better Words For Better Living

Babies' smiles are infectious. We have a new baby in our life. No, not ours. My wife Eleanor's best friend's daughter, Stephanie, has the most pleasant year old cherubim named Charlotte.

Charlotte's smile is so powerful it can give you a positive boost for week. She doesn't have a "toothy" smile, but her smiling eyes more than make up for that. It's her "smiling eyes" that really get you. You know someone is sincere when their eyes are smiling in sync with their face. When she smiles, her face lights up, her eyes shine and she broadcasts a message that says, *"welcome to my world, so come play with me and we can have some fun and fully enjoy our lives."*

Use this word everyday for a week. Check yourself below.							
Sun	M	T	W	T	F	Sat	

Bill Becker

> **Success:** noun: triumph, accomplishment, achievement, star
>
> *What a success story Bill and Melinda Gates turned out to be.*

When I think of success, I think of Bill Peterson, one of my best friends. Occasionally, for my business, I go to a sheriff sale in Philly for abandoned properties. At a sale about 20 years ago, a young, blond haired, blue-eyed man stood beside me and watched me bid. He struck up a conversation and we exchanged cards. His card had all the usual info and words that indicated he was successful real estate investor. He also told me his license plate read SUCCESS.

He had just graduated from a Dale Carnegie Course and he kept using the word success in many of his statements. I also graduated some years before him. Having coached the course several times, I knew the people who attended had integrity.

Bill and I hit it off pretty well during lunch. He also told me that he was interested in a property but was shy five thousand dollars. I know you are going to find this hard to believe. I went to the bank and withdrew the cash and gave it to him. He was the successful bidder and he was ecstatic. He said he would get me the money within a few of days and I believed him. He contacted me the very next day and asked if I could drive down to his mother's house in

Better Words For Better Living

Longport, along the gold coast of New Jersey or if I wanted to wait until he came back to Philly.

I went to his mothers house, a huge old Victorian fronting the ocean, probably worth a half million dollars, in those days. I had dinner with his parents and afterwards, he ushered me in another room. He gave me the money careful not to make the transaction in front of his parents. You knew instinctively they were from old money. That their principle residence was on the main line of Philadelphia seemed to bear this out.

Bill and I became fast friends over the years and still are. My wife and I stayed at his family's place for 5 weeks in Key West Florida at an exclusive resort, and it didn't cost us a dime. In fact I wrote one of my real estate books while I was there. We also stayed at his mother's house many times over the years until his dad passed away.

During one visit, I began talking to his sister and related to her how I got to meet Bill. She said, you were the guy my brother was talking about who was so trusting. And then she shared with me how the family had funded him on many failing business ventures and refused to fund his latest craze, real estate investing. And that's when I entered the picture. For many months, they couldn't figure out how he got started or how he became successful. His sister said he kept telling us he was going to be a success and it happened.

Bill Becker

Are there Bill Petersons in your life? Or are you like him? Do you believe you are a success before you are, despite your friends or family members who don't believe you can do it? If you do, then I can guarantee you will be a success.

Bill believed, and still does. What I believe; is that success can't be purchased or arrived at it, that it is a process of experience. I've felt always welcome whenever I was in his company regardless of what he was doing because of his warm and friendly smile.

Use this word everyday for a week. Check yourself below.						
Sun	M	T	W	T	F	Sat

Better Words For Better Living

> **Terrific:** adjective: super, very good, remarkable, awesome, great, wonderful and excellent
>
> *Every day is terrific when you let God lead you to your dreams and you follow and serve others on the way.*

Terrific is not used as much as it use to be and that is not so terrific. However, I believe it's making a come back, and that would be terrific. Many of us, including me, have come back from something. Every day we, screw up regardless of our egos. Think hard about what you can improve at the end of each day and you will put the ego in its place. Once you get that out of the way, you can concentrate on the terrific things you started or accomplished. This process cleanses the spirit.

I've mentioned before that my late spiritual guide/mentor, Sister Charity, believed the peak learning period for all humans is between the ages of 2 and 7. "Catch them and train them when they are between the ages of 2 &7 and you have them for life," she said. It is most interesting that our court system deems a seven-year-old child is capable of discerning between right and wrong.

We wonder, when children come up with some extremely intelligent comment or remark how they did it. It's almost as if these ideas were programmed into their brain by an unknown powerful force. We know the source of that power, but we need to recognize it. To me, it's the life force of God and I think that's terrific.

My almost three year-old step grandson, (my present wife's daughter's son), is a perfect example. I'll take him for a walk around the block where we live. St Peters Roman Catholic Church is on our little trek. In fact, the church is directly behind the house with some trees and a parking lot in between. You will see how that comes into my little story a bit later.

When my wife Eleanor was still capable, we would both take him with us on our walk and stop by the church. He always got excited because there's a small pond with a couple of dozen gold fish, next to the steps of the church. He loved to watch and sometimes play with them. He called them issues.

When Eleanor became incapacitated, I would walk him there and sometimes take him in the small chapel beside the main church, which was almost always open. Inside, in the stillness, he was in awe of seeing of the sacred sacrament. I would take his little hand and have him bless himself when entering and leaving. When we left I told him we just visited Gods house and this is where God lived. I'd point to the crucifix, which I wear, and say this is God's son. His name is Jesus. Remember now he was just 2 ½ plus years old and could only say a few words. Regardless, I knew he had completely absorbed what was happening.

Anything he didn't understand or was afraid of,

Better Words For Better Living

he called a "Dakus." For example, he called lawnmowers Dakus, because he was afraid of them. Every day, sometimes more than once, he would exclaim Dakus and jump into my arms. We'd go to the back of the house and he'd point to the garage, where the lawnmower was, and say Dakus. I'd say the Dakus is hiding in there.

The back yard was at the back of St Peters. Pointing to the church, I'd ask him, "What's that?" He'd reply, "God lives there" and then point to my cross and say, Jesus. Wow, some would say it's amazing. I think not. It's the mysterious force that we sometimes experience and don't know what to call it. I know and believe this force is God.

There are a lot of terrific happenings going on the world, too many to comprehend. And for me, all these happenings are a prime example of the God force. It's ours to use whenever we wish, as long as we use it for good and the benefit of others.

Use this word everyday for a week. Check yourself below.						
Sun	M	T	W	T	F	Sat

> **Tremendous:** adjective: great, awesome, magnificent, super, superb, marvelous, awesome, fabulous.
>
> *When you arise in the morning and declare, "Today is the day God has made and it will be tremendous," it will certainly be one.*

I listen to a lot of motivation and inspirational talks, at live seminars and on audio recordings. In fact, I have recorded many inspirational and spiritual lectures and have learned from the best people. One particular speaker and inspirational lecturer was a very spiritual man who billed himself Tremendous Jones. His self-promotion worked well and he sold many tens of thousands of recordings.

Tremendous Jones also spoke in person to many hundreds of thousands across the globe. Indeed, he was a tremendous speaker and a real down to earth mover and shaker when it came to getting people stirred up and moving in the right direction. He thought he was tremendous. And guess what — he was.

How about you? Will you get yourself stirred up, get motivated? You know you can by just believing it and summoning the power within you for a little help. Some folks may need a lot of help. Regardless

Better Words For Better Living

of which category you find yourself in, you can be tremendous. If you think you can, you can. But if you think you can't, you can't. Don't quote me on that because it came from one of the most tremendous leaders in our country of the 19th century. He was a man of few words. His name is Abe Lincoln.

Abe's track record was just the opposite of tremendous. It included a nervous breakdown and the loss of every election except the big one. You see, God knew exactly what he was doing when He groomed Abe for the most important job of all time. That job was to create equality among all people. Humanity needs that to happen again throughout the world. As Americans, we are the leaders in this field. Because every nation looks to America for guidance, we must walk our talk all of the time.

What kind of tremendous effect will you have after you have gone ahead to visit your long deceased relatives? Hey, I hit a nerve right? You're probably squirming a bit right? Another tremendous speaker, Jim Rohn said, "The only thing you should leave behind is your pictures and your journal so others can learn from you. But most of all, leave your spiritual guidance, in whatever form that will attract attention in this world."

Picture yourself in the clouds, or wherever you

want. Of course, no one can see you because you are in spiritual form, not your physical self. But your presence and soul is felt by whomever you spiritually encounter. They read what you left and they are curious to see what you looked like and your photos and videos are available for them to go through.

Wow, they say. What an awesome person. You must have been incredible because these writings are marvelous, not necessarily sensational, but certainly remarkable. Maybe you are not an Abe Lincoln or Ghandi, or Martin Luther King. But you did make a positive difference in the world by your actions, all your tremendous actions.

Use this word everyday for a week. Check yourself below.						
Sun	M	T	W	T	F	Sat

Better Words For Better Living

> **Understanding:** adjective: sympathetic, supportive, kind, perceptive, indulgent, considerate, thoughtful and appreciative
>
> *One of the most understanding men I have ever had the pleasure of knowing was my father.*

"It's a Wonderful Life," a great movie with James Stewart and Donna Reed, comes to mind when thinking about understanding. In my opinion, the director Frank Capra embodied many of life's realities and what if it's like to be a good a human being, in all of his films.

James Stewart plays the main character. His mother had a quiet understanding of human nature, especially when he was courting Donna Reed. But it was his father who had the greatest understanding of the world. Whenever he was in doubt about anything, he would turn to his father for advice.

Many parents have this ability and have shared it with their children, friends and people in their sphere of influence. The angel, Clarence, was also an understanding character, but he had others including God to keep him in line. I have watched this movie many, many times and always tear up at the end.

I highly recommend this delightful and insightful movie, not only at Christmas, but also, at any time when you're feeling down. Here's an interesting note about Jimmy Stewart. He portrayed a wise, kind, appreciative person who illustrated the concept of understanding in almost all of the parts he played.

My mother had the privilege to work at the Union League in Philadelphia as a waitress. One night, she came home and showed me a soupspoon. She told me it was the one that Jimmy Stewart used when she waited on him in club's dining room. She also said he was the kindest, most gentle person she had ever waited on anywhere.

We become what our parents and mentors do, not what they say. My father believed this. He was certainly not a saint. He tried to be understanding while raising me. We all learn from teaching others. As I got older, I saw that in everything I attempted to accomplish. Understanding, taking action and following up are the keys to successfully meet any challenge.

We all know understanding people are sometimes taken advantage of. We must be understanding, wise and perceptive in attempting to help others and ourselves. Understanding is similar to mercy or to forgiveness It may be tough for some people to accept understanding as the first step to forgiveness. Being understanding, ready to forgive and take action for the benefit of a person who may have harmed you, will cause a "Feel Good" ray to shine in that person's mind, but more importantly in your mind as well.

Use this word everyday for a week. Check yourself below.						
Sun	M	T	W	T	F	Sat

Better Words For Better Living

> **Utmost:** adjective: highest, extreme, greatest, paramount, supreme maximum and or ultimate
>
> *When he was interviewed, Muhammad Ali, would shout with the utmost audacity, "I am the greatest" andarguably he was.*

I'm not a big boxing fan, but I'll always remember Muhammad Ali. Ali had great self confidence. If you would shout, "I am the greatest," with the utmost of emotion as Ali did, chances are that's what you'd become. Some call it over the top. Others would say, "A person like that was really stuck on himself." And there are some who would make what I call "jealousy statements." I'm sure you probably heard a few of those yourself. However, the truth is that we have not only be stuck on ourselves, we need to be stuck on the task at hand.

Humility plays a big role in building confidence. You must exercise the utmost humility, not only in order to gain confirmation from yourself, but to advance support for yourself as well. You can't achieve the top position in your chosen field entirely by yourself. Think seriously about that statement, because if "you get it," you will be much happier. You'll also find that those around your will extend you the utmost respect,

The most highly respected people in their fields

will readily admit that there was one person, or in many cases, a few people that set them on the path of learning and understanding humility before they became great. This is true in sports, entertainment or political environments. The next task at hand, is to maintain, to the utmost of their strength, that middle ground, neither high nor low, no matter what others say or do.

Many of the superstars of any endeavor will come down crashing very, very hard if they do not maintain an even level or fail to get back up after a defeat. They always ask themselves these questions. "How can I get better? Is this the time I should rethink where I am and where I am going? Am I being very honest with myself? Do I think; things have changed and might it be time for me to change as well?"

All great leaders have pondered these questions. Leaders like Mandela knew their time had come. He remains a powerful icon of freedom. He knew as well as any consummate leader, that if you make the purpose of your existence greater than life itself, you'll succeed. Your success many may not necessarily happen in your time, but it will in His.

Use this word everyday for a week. Check yourself below.						
Sun	M	T	W	T	F	Sat

Better Words for Better Living

> **Valor:** noun: Courage, bravery, spirit, nerve, fearlessness. Valor is derived from the Latin valere, meaning to be strong.
>
> *The many warriors who have fought for the freedom we enjoy are examples of exemplary valor.*

When I think of valor, I think of honor, glory and courage. It takes courage to do what is right, to persist, to never back down. Valor is that fire in your belly that tells you, "I can do it" - I can climb that hill, I can lift that weight, I can overcome that obstacle. Valor is that little voice in the back of your head saying, "never give in, never give in, and never give in!"

Valor is something William Wallace had plenty of. The subject of the movie Braveheart, Wallace had the courage to fight for his convictions against tremendous odds. His goal, to win freedom for his kinsman was thwarted at every turn by powerful and wealthy enemies. However, Wallace kept to his convictions - he would never give in! He would be down in the trenches fighting with his allies risking life and limb in spite of all odds. He refused money and titles, even though both would have let him live a comfortable and secure life. In the end, he even refused a swift and painless death, because it meant compromising his principles and relinquishing his dream of freedom.

Bill Becker

I doubt any of us will have to go to the lengths that Wallace did to support our beliefs. His valor in the face of tremendous challenges is something to emulate. Decide to climb that hill, to lift that weight, to obtain that degree. Whatever the goal is, decide! Valor will give you the strength to ensure your burning desire remains a constant flame in a sea of encompassing night. Though the movie contained fictional elements, it was mostly based on historical knowledge. Regardless, William Wallace was a true visionary of his time.

Use this word everyday for a week. Check yourself below.						
Sun	M	T	W	T	F	Sat

Better Words for Better Living

> **Visionary:** noun: futurist, prophet, creative thinker
>
> *Nelson Mandela is a visionary seeing all nations and peoples being united and free of racial strife. He has invested over 25 years of his life to see this come to a successful completion.*

Your mind is a camera, constantly taking pictures and movies of your life at any given time. Based on these pictures, you envision where you would like to be and share your vision with others. To that end, we're all visionaries. But where are your visions taking you?

Are you envisioning big or small goals? Do your visions include helping others or are they just self-serving? Did you ever volunteer on a committee of a nonprofit or your church? Leaders have visions of what their mission is. What is your mission in life? Think about it.

I have read about the life of a man who was totally devoted to a mission much larger than himself. His name was Gandhi, a true and loyal visionary. His story is good read but the movie of his life, starring the acclaimed actor Ben Kingsley, is even better. Gandhi was true visionary because he remained dedicated to his vision's mission, despite suffering great physical harm inflicted by the governing party under British rule in Africa and India.

He started as an attorney, educated in England, and was an advocate of under represented people who were lacking basic civil rights in Africa of the time. He fought hard for those people and his efforts ultimately changed history in the way people were treated. How's that for a big mission?

Ghandhi didn't stop there. He returned to his homeland, India, and though he suffered brutally under their system, he managed to help change the entire governmental structure leading India to achieve independence. He became a man of the people, wearing a humble white garment woven by hand, made in his native India. He led a march against the government controlled salt mines in India. He started walking to the ocean to get salt instead of buying it from the government. He started that march with a just a few followers. As he walked through the towns, people lined up along the road. Instead of just gawking as he went by, they joined him.

By the time he reached the ocean, newspapers reported that there well over one hundred thousand people. I still get goose bumps whenever I watch that movie, and I have watched it at least 25 times.

To be a visionary, you must first have a vision of what you want. The bigger the better, because if you chose the vision to benefit others, people will get in step with you to help you reach your goal.

Use this word everyday for a week. Check yourself below.						
Sun	M	T	W	T	F	Sat

Better Words for Better Living

> **Welcome:** adjective: admitted gladly and eagerly and delightfully accepted. It can also be used as a noun
>
> *Hospitality and welcome go hand in hand like a newly married couple.*

"Welcome" is a special word. It often answers a need and almost always carries a warm and friendly feeling with no expectation of anything in return. For instance, I welcome any feedback on my books and blogs. It's a way of gauging content so I can best help my readers. I believe most of us don't use the word "welcome" often enough for it to be more useful in our daily lives

Of course, if you took it literally you might interpret it as "come in well." That might be a little strained because that may assume you are not well. Unless of course, if you're a doctor and looking for new business.

If you're in the sales field (and aren't we all), using words with positive meanings is especially useful. I'm sure you've been in a retail store and heard someone approach you and say, "Can I help you?" This greeting must be inviting, friendly and welcoming. If not, the customer will be gone in a flash. It is a more difficult to convey a warm welcome via the telephone and certainly more difficult with the

Internet. But it's possible if we don't want our remarks taken the wrong way.

Giving some thought to how you are going to say anything is extremely vital if you want to increase your happiness in life. You must be satisfied with your welcome and excited to have the person whom you're welcoming to enter into your "inner circle of joy."

Believe me, they will almost immediately know, you're sincere and respond in a like manner. As everyone says, "What goes around, comes around." It is even biblical; 'sow and you shall reap' There is lots of good stuff in that great book. Maybe you should welcome in the new day with a verse or two. I'm sure if you do, you may receive a warm welcome from the Creator when it's time to enter His house.

Use this word everyday for a week. Check yourself below.						
Sun	M	T	W	T	F	Sat

Better Words for Better Living

> **Wonderful:** adjective: magnificent, superb, amazing, fantastic, brilliant, really outstanding or a quality that promotes admiration
>
> *Eleanor what a wonderful person you are to volunteer at the Cathedral Kitchen for the homeless.*

Wonderful is such a wonderful word, it's one of my favorites. We should end our phone conversations with; "Have a wonderful day/evening." Our British friends liken this word to "brilliant" and the upper crust likes to use "splendid." These are all most wonderful words to use when communicating with anyone.

One of my all time favorite, movies which I rank as number one is "It's a Wonderful Life," starring James Stewart and Donna Reed. The movie portrays a man played by James Stewart who grew up in small town America. His dad, a prominent banker of the town, was a wise sage. As a banker who gave the hard working folks an opportunity to own their own homes, he helped many hard working folks build better lives. However, the only other town bank was quite the opposite. The owner of that bank, was a curmudgeon, played by Lionel Barrymore.

After the death of his father, James Stewart took over running the bank and new position was a real PITA to the other banker. Stewart met and married

Donna Reed. They had a slew of kids and were doing fine until a bank error caused him to go into deep despair. He feared that he was going to jail for an employee's mistake and wished had never been born.

He viewed the situation so seriously he was going to commit suicide. During this dark time an angel visited him. When the angel pointed out that without him other lives were negatively affected, he came to the ultimate realization that he indeed had a wonderful life. The entire town would not have existed as it was without his help.

This is a wonderful Christmas story as well as a story for any season whenever you are feeling a little down or just want a lift. It is a wonderful story and not to be missed. Rent it, buy it and absorb it. It's the number one "feel good" movie of all time. Yes, this flick is guaranteed to bring a little joyful tear to your eye and renewed hope for humankind.

Use this word everyday for a week. Check yourself below.						
Sun	M	T	W	T	F	Sat

Better Words for Better Living

> **Xenial:** adjective: amiable to each other, friendly with a host
>
> *At a recent business networking event, there was a definite xenial atmosphere very prevalent that resulted in a xenial community.*

The English language has so many words it is almost impossible to know them all. Xenial, is one of those words that's rarely used, but should be used more often. Perhaps it gets confused with senile and people may be reluctant to use it thinking they could be insulting. It's pronounced with a zee sound. You'll probably need an unabridged dictionary to find "xenial" because most don't include it. I like it because it implies a warm and friendly relationship between hosts and guests and think it would be wonderful if all the communities, the world over, had xenial relationships.

I attend many networking functions. The ones I like attending the most are those that have a xenial feeling. There is one particular person whom I have been friendly with for almost 20 years. Jim R, is an amiable character for the most part, who sometimes "gets on your nerves," but in a good way. If you're in his company, you'll know it. What Jim R does is introduce you to someone whom you may not know. Even if he has only known you for a few minutes, he'll present you as if he were your best friend. Jim R is a xenial character and the entire group becomes happier and more amenable to each other. In all the years I've known him, I never heard him say a bad word about anybody or anything…wow! I actually learned that from him.

For many years, Jim R and I have a sort of competition as which of us is the best dancer. Jim would always have a date, or before he was married, find a woman in the room to dance with him at a charity event or party.

Not to brag but I've been told that I was a pretty good dancer. At many events I've been asked to dance by women who were often 25 years younger than me. So now you know why I felt good about dancing.

Jim R told me he had taken many lessons to master all sorts of dancing. Once the other hand, I just watched really good dancers and imitated them and I do have a sense of rhythm. Many times Jim R and his wife and my wife and I were the only couples on the dance floor usually surrounded by party goers cheering us both. Oh what fun that was.

Though my personality may not be as exuberant as Jim's, I make up for it with my rhythm, feet and body movements. This kind of happiness is infectious and sets the stage for a xenial community wherever you may be. Start utilizing the spirit of the word and the word itself. You will be glad you did.

Use this word everyday for a week. Check yourself below.						
Sun	M	T	W	T	F	Sat

Better Words for Better Living

> **X factor:** noun; hard-to-describe influence or quality; an important element with unknown consequences; also written X-factor
>
> *My friend Chris has told me that I have the X-Factor, an unknown something that he says I possess.*

OK, is this a word? I think so! There was a time when "ain't" wasn't an acceptable word but times change. I'm not really known for certain if X-factor is accepted now, but I do know it's used in many instances and situations. This is particularly true in situations when we're not really sure about something. Like, "Wow, is the true or just conjecture?" The dictionary/encyclopedia says, "X-factor represents something unknown." So let's start from here.

You know when someone has that x factor. It's a certain unexplainable attribute. You'll recognize it in actors—Robert Redford, Meryl Streep and of course Jack Nicholson, and other performers such as Elvis and ole blue eyes Frank Sinatra. Yeah, I know we call it "star power," but nevertheless it is an x-factor that most other individuals don't have. How about authors and poets: Keats, Joyce, and of, course, the most famous of them all, the great bard Shakespeare. Yes they all had that x-factor, wherever derived from, or perhaps as a gift from our Lord. I guess, if we are blessed, we may find out some day but certainly not in this plane.

Some ordinary people and animals possess the

x-factor. Some may walk beside you. You know that there is something different about them but you can't quite ascertain what it is. It's the x-factor! What about the athlete, who no matter what he or she gets involved is very, very good. One is Bo Jackson, a football and baseball star. His gift is the x-factor. Sometimes, we'll say what a talented individual he is. So, is talent the same as the x-factor? That's something to think about isn't it?

All of us have an x-factor. But most people (99%) either don't know what it is, or for varying psychological reasons, never pursue using it. The "it" factor It could be that the "it" factor can also be construed as an x-factor. We've heard that term used in reference to people in entertainment and sports. How then, can we find out what our x-factor is? One way is by asking others how they see us and giving us an unbiased opinion from their perspective? Sure, it's hard to get an honest answer, but it's up to you to interpret what they mean in order to get the real picture..

Ok, enough of the deep stuff. Let's cut to the chase. What's is YOUR x-factor? If you don't know, it's up to you to find IT. At least you know you have one! If you know, then make IT more powerful so you can leave this world a better place than you were born into.

Use this word everyday for a week. Check yourself below.						
Sun	M	T	W	T	F	Sat

Better Words for Better Living

> **Yes:** interjection: all right, agreed, sure, okay, fair enough
>
> *When a long time male companion of a female asks her to marry him, he hopes she says yes.*

Yes, is also one of my favorites. It's so easy to use in everyday conversation. Try this out. Get someone to say yes ten times in a row. In America, a nod of the head or a thumbs means yes. Do you want to get someone to buy into what you are selling? Get them saying yes to all your questions and or comments. Try it. It really works. Ask any good salesperson and they'll tell you — yes, that does work most of the time.

A bank started in New Jersey started a marketing genius, became known as the "YES Bank." In fact, the people who eventually took the bank over still tag it as "YES Bank" even though the name changed. Interesting note is that the bank uses yes in their phone number. People like saying yes, period. Ask an astute politician. They will tell you when they want to get an amendment though to the people they present is as a "yes" or "no" vote. I am sure if you have voted you have seen this strategy without even noticing. Statistics show that no matter what the issue is, the yes question almost always tallies more votes than a no count.

When it comes to the concept of time, yes can be deceiving. Regardless of what we see or hear on the news, all of us want accommodate others. It is in our genome. A Higher Power put it there for the purpose of helping each other. I'm sure you've read, "Love your neighbor as you would yourself." My wife tells me I say yes too many times to projects or people. When this happens I get overwhelmed. That is one of the reasons I go to Vermont and stay with the Benedictine Monks a few times a year. These retreats always help get me charged up, spiritually, physically, mentally and emotionally.

Can you imagine how many times God says yes? You can be sure it's a lot, a whole lot. But keep in mind that's it in His time frame, not ours. So don't get caught up in your zeal for asking. He will take his time and only if it benefits you and others. This is good to remember.

Use this word everyday for a week. Check yourself below.						
Sun	M	T	W	T	F	Sat

Better Words for Better Living

> **Young:** adjective. not very old, youthful, recently started and relatively an early stage.
>
> *Many actors look younger than they are, while others are young at heart because of their positive attitude.*

We all know people who have that glowing, young look and presence regardless of their age. Then there are others who seem a lot older than they really are. I'm sure we all know both kinds of those people. For the moment, let's keep it positive and focus on those youthful peeps.

How about listing those folks you know who look younger and more youthful than their actual ages. That should inspire you to looking young and maintaining a more youthful attitude. It all comes from within you, not from the outside.

I believe in the power within me. I always strive to keep my demeanor and attitude positive, even after quite a few tragedies in my life. Sure, we can attempt to ward off the old age by dressing younger, dyeing our hair or other youthful cosmetic treatments. But when all said and done, it is from deep within that we are young.

I know a woman in her late nineties. If you were to talk to her on the phone or in person and close your eyes, you would think she was in her twenties. Even though she moved a tad slower than someone younger, she appears as being youthful and vibrant.

I don't know much about the acting profession, but I am certain you know of many famous actors who are method actors, like the late Marlon Brando and James Dean. They could literally portray their roles so convincingly; their spouses were often concerned that they would stay in character after the movie/play was finished. My point, course, is that we all can become method actors when it comes to being young. Talk yourself into it. Then act it out with conviction.

How you might say! Believing you are younger can make you feel and act younger. Believing makes it happen and could take years off your actual age. Sure, it may be strange, but what's the difference if it can work for you. Think young and youthful thoughts until your last breath, even if your physical age is 104.

I just heard on the news that the oldest person had just died at 116. Yes, I said, "116." They're countries they call Blue Countries, like Costa Rica, where I have been investing in real estate for over 10 years. The people are friendly. They eat organically and are not afraid of hard work. But more than that, they have the youthful appearance and an inner "something" which is obvious. Their positive attitude and belief system of always willing to help others keeps them young. Their belief in God is their anchor. I attend church services while I'm there. When I go,

Better Words for Better Living

every service is always packed and there's standing room only. I believe this the "key" ingredient in their recipe of always being young. Choose something much larger than you, whether it is God or a Charity that helps people have better lives, and you will enjoy a much better life than you do now.

Remember, to be young—think young!

Use this word everyday for a week. Check yourself below.						
Sun	M	T	W	T	F	Sat

Bill Becker

> **Zeal:** noun: a passion, keenness, eagerness, fervor ardor, fanaticism
>
> *Once you discover your "why,' with the proper planning, implementation and unstoppable zeal, you will make a reality.*

We all know people who demonstrate zeal. In fact, the Bible actually called some Zealots. I am referring to a positive zeal not an extremist zeal. There is controlled zeal in pursuit of your goal as long as it is benefitting all humankind.

Early on in my married years, I befriended a Jewish plumber by the name of Jerry W. Jerry and I worked together when I was in the trades. He was searching for "something spiritual" but not sure of what it was! We had many talks about religions, as I like to do, and still do.

One day, Jerry "got it." He was born again I was happy for him because his whole demeanor changed in a positive way. He was happy and buoyant and joyful. He was displaying great zeal.

One day shortly afterward, he was scheduled to do some minor plumbing work at my home. My wife, Mary, was at home with the children. When Jerry completed his job, he asked Mary for a glass of water and very anxiously proceeded to share his new found joy. Mary said he talked for over an hour.

Better Words for Better Living

That day I was doing some electrical work at another location when I received a phone call from Mary. She was very "agitated". She told me what happened and after an hour lecture by Jerry, he put his hands on her shoulders. He then asked her to kneel to be saved. She refused and told him to leave! And then she called me.

Of course I contacted Jerry and asked him what happened. He related the same events and could not understand why Mary didn't want to be "saved". I knew Mary and what she did not want to do. She wasn't persuaded.

Several months later, Jerry asked me to meet him and have coffee. He explained and apologized for being so zealous when talking to Mary. There's a big difference between exhibiting zeal for what you believe in and "beating someone on the head with a bible" for whatever reason and not just religion.

All religion is good, but we all know there are extremists. It's beneficial to control your zeal. Use your zeal and passion in a way that will propel you to the zenith of your profession and help you achieve your goals.

Use this word everyday for a week. Check yourself below.						
Sun	M	T	W	T	F	Sat

> **Zenith:** noun: peak, summit, top, apex and high point
>
> *JFK was at his zenith, when he was tragically shot by an assassin.*

Many people, both popular and unpopular, were at their zenith when tragedy struck. One of my favorites was Will Rodgers, America's foremost everyone's philosopher. He underscored and portrayed nearly all of the previous positive words with a warm friendly smile and lilt in his voice. Do we know people like him? Sure we do. We like to be around these people or see them on the big or little screen because they affect us in such a positive way. We feel better when they appear!

We all have this hidden power that some call charisma. I know it is a gift from our Power Within. Those around you, affect you regardless of whether those effects are negative, positive or neutral, that is to say, in the middle. If you think you're in the middle about the people around you, dig a little deeper into their character. Think about the way they talk treat and others. These things can be so buried so deeply inside, we may not even know what they are unless we focus on a possible character flaw.

The people around you, those that you regularly associate with, can inadvertently keep you from your

Better Words for Better Living

achieving your personal zenith in your endeavors. At the very least, they make your goal much harder to attain. I know. I was stuck in a relationship once that had those same signals. Because of my emotions and sense of responsibility, I didn't recognize it until a crisis developed. That is when the proverbial mud hit the fan!

But you know, once the crisis was over, I fell right back into the same trap again and again. I withdrew into a personal comfort zone and ignored all the signals. Does that sound familiar to you? Do you want to reach your zenith or are you stuck in the middle?

This is an appropriate question for our last positive word because it will affect your entire life from this point forward. If you need to make a change, hard as it may be, in the company you keep, you must do it immediately. That's when you will begin to grow and move quickly to approach your personal zenith. And that's an iron clad, bulletproof guarantee!

Use this word everyday for a week. Check yourself below.							
Sun	M	T	W	T	F	Sat

Some Final Words

Conclusion or the beginning of a new life?

This is my third book and my first two books "The Power Within:A spiritual journal," and my second book. "Setting and Getting your Goals," was combined to become "The Brink of Bankruptcy," which addresses different forms of bankruptcy. So I have titled this book *"Better Words for Better Living"*. Unlike my other two books, this one only took 3 years to write not 15.

When you follow this system of using a positive word each week for a year I guarantee your life will change or the better. There are many more positive words in the English language but I have just chosen these as words to include in your daily life to help make each day a little better than the one before. Each word is accompanied by a short mini essay on various subjects which relate to that word. I hope you enjoy!

The Last Word

> **Hear:** verb: make out, listen to, sit in judgment, perceive sounds, be informed, understand, to get to know something
>
> *I'd like to hear from you!*

Well, now that you've heard from me, I'd like to hear from you. If you have a special personal power word that works for you, a unique life experience you'd like to share, or even if you just feel like giving me some feedback or saying hello, I love to hear from you. You can send your comments or thoughts directly to me using the link below to **MyPower Within** website:

http://www.mypowerwithin.com/contact/html

You can also reach me toll-free at: 1.800.331.0202
Looking forward to hearing from you soon.
Bill Becker

About the Author

A resident of Philadelphia for more than 60 years, Bill has been an instructor and guest lecturer at Temple and Drexel Universities, has conducted classes in real estate investment at community colleges throughout the Delaware Valley, as well as a guest speaker and instructor for many nationally know real estate investment programs and clubs across America. He has taught or consulted over 10,000 students over the course of his carest in the real estate investment field. Bill has authored 5 real estate investment books and recorded over 18 educational and motivational CDs.

As Chairman of CORA a nonprofit agency which helps nearly 18,000 children and families every year, Bill spends a lot of time giving back since Cora's inception over 45 years ago. Bill is also very involved in the PEW Foundation's Inglis House, which is home to over 300 residents with various physical challenges. He serves on the board of The Starting Point, started by Vincent De Pasquale, another nonprofit located in New Jersey, dedicated to the marginal denizens of society.

Bill is the founder and president of the American Real Estate Institute (AREII), a company specializing in the education of real estate investors

About the Author

throughout the Delaware Valley Tri-Sate area (PA, NJ DE). AREII teaches real estate investments through intensive training programs, network mentoring, and specialized programs for investors interested in specific real estate strategies such as, sheriff sales, tax sales foreclosures, lease options, rent-to-own, and discounted mortgages. As a well-known lecturer and instructor, Bill is widely recognized as an exemplary trainer of trainers. As an investor, Bill has dealt with hundreds of properties, with a portfolio consisting of large commercial properties and residential units.

Author of the highly successful "Brink of Bankruptcy," and "The Power Within," Bill conducts symposiums and seminars to his many thousands of students and the general public. He holds 2 hour, 1 and 2 day workshops on the inner workings of the powerful concepts covered in the books. In addition, he conducts an annual retreat at the Weston Priory in Vermont, where he takes a limited amount of people for a week for a spiritual pilgrimage.

Bill continues to be a highly sought after lecturer in the Philadelphia and South Jersey Metropolitan areas. Contact him though his websites, email or phone.

http://www.areii.com
http://mypowerwithin.com
Bill@areii.com or 1.800.331.0202

www.ingramcontent.com/pod-product-compliance
Lightning Source LLC
Chambersburg PA
CBHW050556300426
44112CB00013B/1943